THE BLOODY THIRD

Mayhem, Murder and Memories of Millville's Third Ward

by

Eileen Bennett and Nelson Trout

Published by: Fireside Publications
Oxford, Florida

The Bloody Third

This book is not a work of fiction. Rather, it is a creative non-fiction story of how the third ward of one New Jersey City grew to garner the nick-name of *The Bloody Third.* Through the years some records have been lost, newspaper archives have a limited lifespan, and memories have dimmed. Because of some of the tragedies retold here, many of the names have been omitted. But the authors have worked tirelessly to verify locations, names and any other facts through police records, N.J. Department of Correction records, or newspaper articles and the memories of people who lived the stories or descendants to whom the stories have been retold, and accept full and complete responsibility for the content contained herein. All pictures are used with the written consent of the Copyright holder and/or the subject of the photo.

Published by:
Fireside Publications
5144 Harbour Drive
Oxford, Florida 34484

http://firesidepubs.com

Printed in the United States of America

First Edition: January 2016

ISBN: 978-1-935517-35-1

For multiple copies of this book visit:
http://firesidepubs.com or
Contact the authors @
ebchristianna@gmail.com

Foreword

In the interest of full disclosure, authors Nelson Trout and Eileen Bennett both lived in the Third Ward for several years in the early 1980s. They resided on Archer Street, near R.D. Wood School – although they never met each other until decades later. The early '80s were a pocket of time during which young professionals and newlyweds moved into the old houses and duplexes and renovated them. Flower gardens suddenly appeared. Children played in the neighborhood.

Unfortunately, recent times have not been kind to the Third Ward. Once filled with charming, gingerbread-tinged duplex houses for the cotton and glass workers, many houses now are vacant or in desperate need of repair. Some have been razed, so the streets look like smiles with missing teeth. Violent crime is not uncommon.

Acknowledgements

Many thanks to: Dale and Joann Wettstein, Robert Francois, Terry Pangburn, Deirdre Walsh Fedkenheuer, Matt Christy, "Coach" Ed Andrews, Jody Farabella, Ethan Aronoff, Lynne Porreca Compari, Jim Quinn, Lorraine Zuccato, Michelle Wright-Hinson, Ken Butcher, Ken Robinson, Christopher Haas, Sara Williams, George Romer, Kurt Hess, Everett John Hoffman, Eleanor Cain, Jane and Matt Christy, Larry Haas, Pat Caruso, Joyce Vanaman, Earl Gramlich, The Press of Atlantic City, The Daily Journal, The News of Cumberland County, Lois Hider, The (now defunct) Bridgeton Evening News and Millville News, D. Renne Brecht, Bonnie Reynolds, Suzy Schwegel, Dennis Schwegel, Martin Schwegel, Gregory Schwegel, Carol Schwegel, D. Renee Brecht, Kem Salvo, Gustav Schick, the late Delbert Brandt, Randolph Brandt, Judi Grau Shute, Kathy Farrell, Brian Kutner, Barry Smith, Donald Shelton, Dr. Richard Beck, Patti Clark Kears, Sue Hinson Marshall, Fran Menz, Bill McClintock, Joe P. Smith, Pat Witt, Elaine Hilliard, Suzy Stiegel, Patti Clark Kears, Maryjane Lloyd Moats, Linda Morgan, Kurt M. Warner, Michele Kirksey, Gay Taylor, Doris Tomlin, Jackie Menz Abbott, Kathy Horseman, Michelle Wright-Hinson, Eleanor Cain, Gladis Rhubart Mcgraw, Lois Crowley, Andy Stover, Micki Gilbert Merritt, Eric Conova, Sonny Craner, Eleanor Cain, Bonnie Reynolds, Vanessa J Moats-Maslowski, Gloria Treen McKenzie, Rose Golden, JoAnn Wyjadka Candy, Carol Uminski Rose, Mary Jane Moats, and Rev. David Ennis.

Acknowledgements cont.

Our thanks also go out to Vanessa J. Moats-Maslowski, Keith Mitchell, Newell Branin, Liz Aridit Caruso, Robert Abbott, Anna Klawitter Sooy, Carole Barber, Harry Fisher, Fran Hovermann, Adrienne Treadway Shorter, Charles "Chick" Bennett, Kathy Powell Horner, Bill Haas, Greg Geraci, George Romer, Alan Shaw, Doug Larosa, Linda Morgan and family, Jeff Trout, John Lookabaugh, Diane Rene Howard-Kuppel, Judith Breeden McFarland, Jamie Baird, Paula Simpkins Maitre, Chrissy Jeffery, Kathy Powell Horner, Newell Branin Jr., James Quinn, Sue Hinson Marshall, Michele Kirksey, Gay Taylor, Doris Tomlin, Jackie Menz Abbott, Mary Marie Terzes, Cheryl Ennals, Bill McCormick, Maggie Marshall Benevento, Michelle Wright-Hinson, Paul McIsaac, Steve Felice, Mary Marie Stites, Cheryl Justice, Harry Fisher and Kathy Powell Horner.

Also a special thank you to the Facebook sites:

"Millville Memory Lane;"
"Born and Raised in Millville's Bloody Third Ward, and *"Cumberland County, N.J. News, Info and Chat,"*

which allowed us to garner essential contacts from former Third Warders from all over the world.

Table of Contents

<u>**CONTENTS**</u><u>: con't.</u>:

PART TWO
Optimistic Revival

PART THREE
Tidbits

Preface

Whenever possible we have tried to verify stories from long ago with police records, N.J. Department of Correction records, or newspaper articles. However, many records have been lost through time, and newspaper archives only go back so far. Therefore, we have had to depend on the memories of people who lived the stories or the children or grandchildren to whom the stories have been passed down. In addition, street addresses have changed with the time, so exact locations may be confusing. In every instance, we have tried to verify locations, names and any other facts. We must remember, however, that memories dim with time, and vary through the passage from one generation to another. Many of the stories printed here were passed down through family lines. Because some of the relatives of the tragedies retold here are still living, out of respect, we have declined to use names.

Following a spate of fatal shootings in 2014, one weary Church Street resident told a reporter for The South Jersey Times, "It's turning into worse than the Bloody Third."

Things may be looking up for the Third Ward, however, as the city proclaims it is taking an unusually aggressive approach to cleaning it up and hopefully returning it to its former neighborly grandeur. We will touch on all these subjects in this book.

Eileen Bennett and Nelson Trout

Dedication

This book is dedicated to veteran community journalist Joyce Vanaman, who covered the city of Millville for The Press of Atlantic City for 40 years. If it happened in Millville, you can be sure Joyce covered it. She is not only a well-respected, compassionate and ethical journalist, but was a mentor to many young reporters (including myself, Eileen Bennett), and has volunteered thousands of hours to various causes in her beloved adopted city. She is an institution unto herself.

This book also is dedicated to all the long-time Third Ward residents, past and present. Their generosity in sharing their stories, memories and photos was truly amazing.

Part One

The Bloody Third

Introduction

For as long as any self-respecting Millvillian can remember, there is a certain section of the city that has always been known as *"The Bloody Third."* Even today, natives from that area proudly declare:

"I'm from the Bloody Third!"

As grim as the moniker may sound, residents wear it as a kind of badge of honor. In this book, we investigate how the *Bloody Third* earned its name, and why it is a source of pride.

Birth of the Third

Millville, New Jersey's Third Ward is noted for baseball, the American flag and apple pie. It just doesn't get any more American than that. Of course, there *were* the murders and ensuing mayhem.

Don't believe it? Well, Mike Trout, arguably the best baseball player today has his roots in the *"Bloody* Third Ward." It's where his great-grandfather, John "Bat" Trout, also a well-known slugger in his day, played baseball.

Now, if that's not quite enough Americana for any of you,

Brothers Robert and Richard Abbott, bakers in the military, opened the most popular bakery in Millville when they returned home. They lived on W. Green St. from 1924-1928.

Photo courtesy of Dale Wettstein.

how about this tiny tidbit of history? The first flag planted on the surface of the moon was partially made from cloth at the old Millville cotton and dye mill. And the apple pie? Well, now! There were these two young Abbott boys, brothers, both from the Third Ward, who would later establish a bakery that became famous with all the local residents as well as others in the area. Their apples pies, so we're told, were *to die for*.

The Bloody Third
By: Eileen Bennett & Nelson Trout

As for the murder and mayhem – well, those tales might be a bit more complicated. Let's just say, the neighborhood earned the nickname *"The Bloody Third"* for a variety of reasons – none of them good.

In the beginning, back in the 1600s, the peace-loving Lenne Lenape Native Americans settled in Millville and other southern New Jersey towns, blessed with pristine forests hugging the marshes and rivers. The City of Millville was incorporated in 1866. The city was geographically divided into five wards.

"Overview of Millville's "Bloody Third Ward."

We interviewed countless people hoping to discover the true history of how Millville's Third Ward earned its dubious nickname. We found a few *facts,* but mostly we found a myriad of people happily retelling tales of their childhood growing up in the Third Ward, and of stories their parents and grandparents told them.

Many kind people shared their stories, anecdotes and even photos of growing up in the Third Ward. It seems there is no shortage of theories as to why the Third Ward was *bloody* – many theories included the rowdy, exhausted glass workers coming off shift; while others included dirty politics, and even the slaughterhouses located there. Religious friction also had its presence in the area – the Catholics versus the Protestants.

There was the Second Methodist Church and:

*The original Second Methodist Church
  At Church and McNeal streets.*   *Photo courtesy of Dale Wettstein*

The Catholic Church, St. Mary Magdalen.

*St. Mary Magdalen Catholic Church on Buck Street was
the only other church in the Third Ward besides the
Second Methodist Church. The rectory is attached.*

And neither faith was supposed to mingle with the other.

Some people claim it wasn't until the turn of the century that the Third Ward became known as the *"Bloody Third."* How this once-peaceful land earned its nickname is difficult to nail down, but there is no shortage of myths. Many old-timers blame it on the glass workers slinging back a few drinks after their long shifts ending in raucous bar fights. Some go one step further, and say the monotonous shift-work, combined with the many taverns in town, predictably ended in domestic violence when the men returned home.

Then there are the tales of unspeakable horror: Crimes and tragedies so heinous they are burned into the memories of *Third Warders* today. We'll explore these tragedies through the eyes of people who lived them, and through stories handed down from the initial *Third-Warders* to their descendants.

The Bloody Third
By: Eileen Bennett & J. Nelson Trout

The infamous Church Street house where the murders Took place in 1917.

Many former, and present, Third Warders point to the story of the infamous *Porreco* family massacre in 1917, as the basis for the nickname *"Bloody Third."* We'll revisit the bloody scene of the *Porreco* murders later, in greater detail.

Growing Pains

When Millville was first incorporated as a city, the cotton mills and the ironworks were the main source of employment, under the auspices of the Richard D. Wood family. The Smith and Wood Iron Foundry, and the New Jersey Mills were constructed in the early 1850s. Ten years later, a bleachery and dye house were added to New Jersey Mills. Together, they would later become the Millville Manufacturing Company.

*The cotton mill on Columbia Avenue
during work shift change.*

The Woods' family prospered in Millville during the 1800s. They had signed a contract with City Council to provide the citizens of Millville with water from their manmade *Union Lake*, which was formed by the construction of a large dam.

The *R.D. Wood and Co. Foundry* was erected in 1814. There, cast iron items were smelted; the idea and usefulness of the products quickly caught on, both for home and business use, thus allowing the Foundry to grow from a relatively small enterprise to a major industry.

R. D. Wood soon became interested in the science of cast-iron pipe production. In short order, this foresighted business man brought his idea to fruition and before long, the Millville furnace was producing cast iron pipe. According to historians, the Wood factory produced and sold the first cast iron pipe sold in the United States.

Millville's ironworks produced many of those iconic, elegant wrought-iron balconies in the New Orleans' French Quarter. Liz Aridit Caruso can attest to that.

"We were in the Garden District of New Orleans admiring the old houses," she said, "and noticed that quite a large number of them had wrought iron railings which were stamped Millville Iron Works, Millville, N.J.!"

The glassworks, for which Millville eventually won fame, would come somewhat later. Because of the abundance of pure silica sand, the glass industry would not only blossom, it would explode. The Third Ward's famous cotton mill, established by R. D. Wood as the Millville Manufacturing Company in 1852, later would hold a distinction in its own right.

Few people know there is a bit of Millville on the moon. In fact, it's been there for years. Neil Armstrong planted the American flag on the moon's surface in the first monumental Apollo 11 moon landing on July 20, 1969. Armstrong famously declared on live television, "one small step for man, one giant leap for mankind," with the red-white-and-blue American flag in the background.

According to local historian Dale Wettstein, the red cloth stripes in the American flag planted on the moon by Armstrong in 1969 were dyed at the Millville cotton mill. (Experts believe that flag – and subsequent flags planted on the moon – are still flying, although the colors likely have faded to white.) Robert Francois, head of the Millville Historical Society, said although the cotton mill and iron works at one time were the blue-collar heart of the city, they eventually were joined by the city's famed glassworks, with Whitall Tatum leading the way in 1857. Many of the workers for all these industries resided in the Third Ward. The mill and glass workers sent their children to the *R.D. Wood School* (named after Millville founder Richard Wood). First came the Irish immigrants, followed by the Italians, all looking for a stable life with a steady job for their families.

The Third Ward was predominately white, according to historian Bob Francois.

"Back in the '50s," he said, "there really weren't any blacks in the Third Ward. Only one out of ten Millvillians were black." African Americans in Millville stayed on the East side. It wasn't a matter of segregation, according to Francois.

"They wanted to stay in their own neighborhood. They built their church in that area (Bethel AME Church at Fifth and Garrison streets.) They didn't have cars. They had to walk to church and to go downtown. They were a real minority here (the Third Ward)," Francois said.

The workers settled near the cotton and wood mills, and the names of the streets reflect the important people of the time: Green Street was named after the superintendent of the cotton mill.

McNeal Street was named after James McNeal, superintendent of the iron factory.

Some street names were self-explanatory: North Street marked the northern border of the city; Church Street was named after the Second Methodist Church, a major house of worship there; Depot Street and Dock Street also were self-explanatory.

Archer Street was named after Isaac Archer, who came to Millville as an ironworker in the employ of the Wood family. Mr. Archer was considered to be a mechanical genius, and thus had a street named after him.

The Bloody Third
By: Eileen Bennett & Nelson Trout

Isaac Archer is credited with straightening the defective standpipe which supplied Millville with water from Union Lake. He is Archer Street's namesake. He is also credited with building the boiler which powered the first steam boat to navigate the Maurice River. The boat itself was built by Isaac Dougherty and launched in 1872.

The Millville and Glassboro Railroad Company was incorporated on March 9, 1857. The Cape May and Millville Railroad Company was incorporated on March 9, 1863. Both these routes would prove to be invaluable in Millville's development. It was a time when the horse-and-buggy was the main mode of transportation. Cushing and Sheppard wrote of Millville:

"The roads and streets were always bad, and at times almost impassable, owing to the depth of the loose white sand which covered the site of the town. They were in their best condition when frozen."

People initially didn't realize that the sandy roads would prove to be a river of gold for the sand industry. South Jersey was considered to have the finest silica sand, the main ingredient in glass-making, in the country.

Cushing and Sheppard also note:
"By Feb. 26, 1866, to take effect March 1, 1866 the whole township of Millville was incorporated in the city of Millville

and divided into three wards. All that part lying south of the Bridgeton and Millville turnpike on the west side of the river, and all on the east of the river south of Main Street and the Leaming Mill road was made the First Ward.

All that part lying east of a line running from Main Street up Buck Street to Cinder (now Broad) Street, then along the centre of that street to the centre of the Millville Glassboro (now West Jersey) Railroad and then northward along that road to the line of Landis Township was made the Second Ward."

Almost as an afterthought, Cushing and Sheppard ended their summary of the town wards by stating: "All the remaining part of the city was made the Third Ward."

The glass industry and cotton mill would change the Third Ward's unimportant image, making it a lively, thriving neighborhood to the hundreds of workers in both those fields. The "Third Ward" was no longer an afterthought. It would become a world of its own, a home to shift workers, handymen and homemakers, among others.

Near the middle of the eighteenth century, the Wheaton family joined Whitall-Tatum in the glass industry in Millville's third ward. Wheaton's entry into Millville's glass industry,

Workers at Flint Tank #12, Whitall-Tatum Company, Making bottles for the drug industry.

Photo courtesy of Dale Wettstein

according to the book, *Millville Glass: The Early Days*, by Virgil S. Johnson, caused the industry to flourish from the mid-1800s, eventually becoming one of the leading employers in the Cumberland County area.

"George S. Bacon was a large man, six feet, two or three inches tall. A short black beard and erect posture helped to give him a dignified appearance. A Quaker, born in Bacon's Neck, Cumberland County in August 1864...."

True to his Bio, George was a man to be reckoned with. He was placed in charge of the Philadelphia branch of Whitall-Tatum in 1888; in 1892, he was named head of the company's Glasstown plant. And in 1894, he was made superintendent of both plants. Truly, George was a man on the move.

Meanwhile, the Millville Manufacturing Co., a cotton mill on the edge of the Maurice River, was completed in 1854.

A view of the cotton mill from the Maurice River.

The cost of the mill and two machines was $250,000, with an additional $100,000 needed to put it into operation. The two massive industries, the cotton mill and the glass trade, would be the source of income for many Third Warders for generations yet to come.

Cushing and Sheppard note:

"Between five hundred and six hundred workers are employed at these works, producing annually about six million pounds of glass, of an approximate value of $300,000."

One can only guess how much that figure would be in today's economy.

The Glassworks

Millville, named after the many mills in town, would become so famous for its glass that Pulitzer-prize-winning poet Carl Sandburg wrote about it in 1905. Sandburg actually lived in Millville for a short time. The poet and author was appalled at the lack of child labor laws, and how children were forced to work in the glass houses. Sandburg wrote:

> *"Down in southern New Jersey, they make glass. By day and by night, the fires burn on in Millville and bid the sand let in the light. Millville by night would have delighted Whistle, who loved gloom and mist and wild shadows. Great rafts of wood and big, brick hulks, dotted with a myriad of lights, glowing and twinkling every shade of red. Big black fumes, shooting out smoke and sparks, bottles, bottles, bottles, of every tint and hue, from a brilliant crimson and other dull green that marks the death of sand and birth of glass."*

It all sounds very romantic – but there was a tragic downside to the glass industry, Sandburg wrote.

Charles Pepper, 80, bottle maker, hard at work at T.C. Wheaton Glass Co.

The Bloody Third
By: Eileen Bennett & Nelson Trout

Local historian, the late Delbert Brandt, in his Vineland Daily Journal column, noted that Sandburg wrote about both the good and bad sides of the glass industries.

"A man with nothing hailing from nowhere can get an easy job at fair pay. Indeed," Sandburg wrote, "the glass blowers' union is one of the most perfect organizations in the country."

While the glass industry may have been an employment blessing, it was a curse for many young boys. The glass blowers made good pay, but they depended on young boys to carry the bottles to different places in the plant. The youngsters were known as the "carryin' boys," and ranged in age from nine to fourteen. These were boys who should have been in school. To say they were exploited would be a monument to understatement. They would work up to ten hours a day for meager wages.

Sandburg described a haunting image of these "carryin' boys." He wrote:

> Passing back and forth in the pale, weird light, these creatures are imps in both the modern and old-time sense of the word. They are grimy, wiry, scrawny, stunted specimens, and in cuss words and salacious talk, they know all that grown men know. In the use of the ever surviving, if not ever fitting superlative, 'damnedest,' they are past masters all.
>
> Their education has consisted mainly of the thoughts, emotions and experiences that resulted from contact with 'blowers' and 'gaffers,' besides views of big barn-like space lit up by white-hot sand. This has been their universe at those times of day when they were most alive, most wide-awake, most sensitive to impressions. The manufacturers have endowed a night-school, The Workman's Institute, but (the teacher told me) the boys cannot keep their heads up, eyes open during sessions, therefore their brains don't make much headway.

Francois noted that child labor laws were nonexistent at the time. Nonetheless, glassmakers tried to help both their workers and the boys who worked for them. Whitall Tatum established the *Working Man Institute* at the foot of High Street, which would later become City Hall and then the police department before it was razed in the early 1980s. It was supposed to provide a place for the workers to socialize and for the boys to get an education.

The original Working Man's Institute, which later became City Hall,, and then the Police Department. Note the flag pole painter and the sign across the building: "The City That Pays As It Goes."

Photo courtesy of Dale Wettstein

According to Cushing and Sheppard's account, a cornerstone for the Institute was laid in July 1882, with "*the whole town joining in a holiday on the occasion.*"

Completed in 1883, its main purpose was supposedly to provide Millville residents a place to read, exercise and watch shows. But even back then the real, unspoken reason for the

Institute was to give men an alternative to the many taverns they frequented after their long shifts.

Cushing and Sheppard hinted at the real reason for the Workman's Institute:

"The various temperance organizations use it as their meeting room, and the Sunday afternoon temperance meetings of the Women's Christian Temperance Union are held there. The audiences are largely from a class which rarely attends a temperance meeting in a church."

Still, Francois said, the Institute did provide men a place where they could exercise in the gym, and boys could attend school classes. There was only one problem, Francois said:

"After working 12 hours, the children would fall asleep in the classrooms."

While the *Working Man's Institute*'s intentions were good, they were unrealistic. Exhausted men wouldn't really feel like exercising after working long monotonous nights. Many would be finishing up their shifts in the early morning hours, as other people were just beginning their work days.

One can only imagine the devastating effect this social/work routine had on family life during this difficult time period. Days and nights were not only turned around for the men – families also had many adjustments to make – allowance had to be made for the workers to sleep during the daytime, often with mothers assuming more responsibility for children and maintaining the household; preparing meals at odd hours, and at times, even dealing with an intoxicated spouse at home. One wonders how family life ever survived in such a climate.

Bars cropped up like dandelions around the Third Ward. Men found a cold beer much more appealing than exercising after a long night. The ritual was so common, police acclimated themselves to it.

Lois Crowley said she remembers her father talking about his father, Leon S. Whilden,   who was a Millville Police Officer in the 1920s.

"My father said he would bring '*drunks*' home to sleep it off on his sofa, "Crowley said, "and take them home the next morning, instead of arresting them,".

Photo courtesy of Lois Crowley

Before becoming a police officer," Lois said. "Leon S. Whilden was the trolley conductor."

Moonshine and Speakeasies

It's hard to argue that the National Prohibition Act – also known as the Volstead Act – was not very popular with the blue-collar working man. The act was created to enforce The Eighteenth Amendment, which prohibited the imbibing of alcoholic beverages of any kind.

There seemed to be no shortage of "moonshine stills" that cropped up in the woods surrounding the Third Ward. Speakeasies – which might be something as primitive as an old, abandoned railroad car – served alcoholic beverages in a "social setting." All of this was hush hush, of course. The word "speakeasy" was merely a way of telling people to speak in whispers, or "easy" tones, so that their covers wouldn't be blown. The exact location of these stills and speakeasies in Millville are but mere rumors and myths today. It seems they held their secrets well.

However, searching the news archives, there seems to have been a pattern of arrests of Third Ward men for "larceny from the Millville Manufacturing Company" and "violation of the prohibition enforcement act." One might speculate these men were stealing from their bosses so they could buy illegal booze.

Indeed, a Third Ward myth says that a Millville industry can lay claim to "inventing" the word "booze." According to Larry Haas, "One of my history teachers was Dr. Elizabeth Bacon. Her family was somehow connected to Whitall Tatum, and she would often talk about the company. The one story I remember best is that Whitall Tatum produced a bottle for use by a Dr. Booze, with his name stamped on the bottom. Dr. Booze's concoction was mainly alcohol, so that's how the *Booze bottle* got its name."

History buff, Terry Pangburn, points to a different take on the "booze" story. He points to a book by John A. Rossi, titled "A Brief History of Glassmaking (and its impact on Southern New Jersey." In it, Rossi writes: "Bottles (or flasks) manufactured in Glassboro, and shaped like a log cabin were used to symbolize the candidacy of William Henry Harrison in the 1840 presidential campaign. The bottles were filled by a Philadelphia druggist named E.C. Booz and soon became known as 'Booz bottles' – popularizing the term 'booze' for whiskey."

With Prohibition in full swing by the 1920s, G-Men were scrambling to crack down on violators. According to at least one news account, their efforts were all but futile. A Jan, 20, 1920 article reported:

"There are all sorts of whisky receipts in the air. Everybody is taking a fling at making the stuff and some of the moonshine product is very, very strong, if all stories are correct. It's going to be some time before the Federal agents succeed in killing the moonshine habit, especially when a popular monthly magazine devotes considerable space, and a number of photographs, to contrivances used to make the stuff, and describes the methods."

Men weren't alone in their quest to satisfy the thirsty. It was not unusual at all for women to supplement the family's income by devising their own "recipe." for "hooch." One Third Ward resident said:

"My grandmom used to brew it in a secret room behind her bedroom. She did whatever she had to do to raise two little girls on her own."

And, by the way, the woman added:

"The cops and even the mayor would buy the stuff. Not a bad idea, huh?"

Even before Prohibition, speakeasies thrived throughout the city. A Bridgeton Evening News article dated Feb. 21, 1914, screamed:
"Police Raid Alleged Speakeasy."

Apparently there was a raid in a speakeasy in the rear of the Giuffra building on High Street. Two men were arrested. "A gallon of rum was found and a jug containing another half-gallon, while there were a dozen or so half pints about the room. About that many cases of beer were in the room."

In yet another article, it was reported:

"Marshal Charles Biggs took Salvatore Remmano into custody last evening, charged with keeping a speakeasy. Remmano conducts a grocery store on Broad Street, one door from Buck Street, and has, it is said, been conducting the speakeasy connected with it."

Home Sweet Home

Housing for the workers was a blessing. According to Cushing and Sheppard,

"The old-time rows of frame tenement-houses, so well known in former years as a marked characteristic of towns where the manufacture of glass was a leading occupation, are no longer built; and the former ones are disappearing. In their places neat, single and double houses are building, with many of the porticos and verandas that have contributed to change Millville from a sandy, uninteresting glass house town, to a neat, well-built attractive city."

Women and girls were not exempt from grueling working conditions in the cotton mills that dominated the city for years.

Many members of the *fairer sex* had to slave along with their husbands, doing *light* work, to keep their family homes. Many of the workers lived in company housing located in the Third Ward. Instead of cash pay, they were indebted to the company store for their groceries, so

Employee Egnac Cyelen is in the spinning room
Of the cotton mill in the late 1940s.

they had markers instead of money for salary. If the men workers spent what little money they had for liquor, one can easily see how an unpleasant domestic life might have evolved. Now, mind you, this was before the temperance movement came into full swing, and before Prohibition was enacted. But it undoubtedly contributed to the volatile atmosphere that marked many homes in the feisty Third Ward. And, that, at least in large part, was responsible for the forming of a chapter of the Women's Christian Temperance League.

According to Lorraine Zuccato, her mother, who grew up in the Third Ward during the 1940s and 50s, told her there was no shortage of bars.

"People would frequent them when they finished their shift at the factories," Zuccato said. "As luck would have it, too much booze usually turns people ugly, therefore fighting occurred. That's why it's called the '*Bloody Third*.'"

Hell's Half Acre and Politics

Terry Pangburn, 71, a retired Cumberland County Sheriff's Officer, is an avid aficionado of Millville history. Although he only lived in the Third Ward from 1976 to 1977, he has done extensive research on the area. Like many others, he points to politics as one of the starting points for the colorful *"bloody"* moniker. "Democrats always got, massacred on

A young couple caught canoodling on the Sharp Street Bridge.

Election Day," in The Third Ward, which was basically Republican. They said the Democrats couldn't buy a vote in the Third Ward." The people maybe could have been Republican at heart, but there was just a certain grittiness about their blue-collar lifestyle, which revolved around the glass houses, the cotton mill, and of course, the bars.

Photo courtesy of Dale Wettstein

"The Third Ward," Pangburn said, "was always the black sheep of Millville."

According to newspaper accounts, the Third Ward was home to *"Hell's Half Acre,"* on Dock Street, which, it was reported, "would disgrace the lowest haunts of Chicago." There, on Dock Street, a woman by the name of Annie Wren was the "proprietress" of a dubious establishment known as *Hotel de Hell's Half Acre*. According to news accounts, it reportedly was a cross between a *speak-easy* and a *house of ill repute*. There are conflicting reports of where *Hell's Half Acre* was located. Some say it was located on Columbia Avenue. But everyone agrees it was in the Third Ward.

The Third Ward wasn't the only section of town in which questionable activities occurred. They all had colorful names: *The Black Diamond*; *The Hen Roost*; *The Evening Star*; and *Yellow Hell* (better known by the locals as 'Yella Hell')." The latter, located on the river near City Hall, was so named because the buildings, oddly enough, were for some unknown reason – mostly painted yellow.

The Millville News reported that

"Drunken brawls, which usually end in shooting(s), are frequent at all these dens." Third warders were known to frequent these places.

Union Lake and Luna Park

Commuter transportation into and out of the city arrived when the first trolley rolled into town on August. 1, 1893. It was an open-aired trolley, which entered into Millville by way of the huge bluffs which overlooked Sharp Street, and then harnessed the flow of Union Lake.

The trolley provided the only transportation in the city other than horse and buggy. It traveled from Millville to Bridgeton, and back.

Photo courtesy of Dale Wettstein

In 1940, that manmade lake, created to provide industrial power to the cotton mill, unexpectedly proved to be a threat to the city. There are just a very few people today who recall the 1940 flood of Union Lake. According to many historical accounts, the water rose four feet above its normal level.

The Sharp Street Bridge at the Union Lake Canal, circa 1960.

The Bloody Third
By: Eileen Bennett & Nelson Trout

It was Labor Day – **a** holiday weekend. Back then, there were no floodgates on the canal, and residents watched in trepidation as the water spilled over into what was then known as *Union Lake Park*. The water inched its way across Sharp Street along Columbia Avenue.

Andy Stover recalls how his dad joined in with all the other people in town to offer their help in the huge sand-bagging operation that needed to be stretched from *Union Lake* all the way across Broad St., up to Millville Manu-facturing Company.

The boat houses at Union Lake Park were a summer refuge for children throughout the city, and especially for those in the Third Ward.

The townspeople were successful in keeping the flood at bay. It was typical of the time back then – when, even on a holiday – neighbors would rally for the good of their community.

While Union Lake was created primarily to provide hydroelectric power to the cotton mill and bleachery, it also provided an oasis in the sweltering heat of summer for Third Ward children. Technically, it was only partially located in the Third Ward. But so much of the Third Ward's life revolved around Union Lake, we decided to devote a chapter to it.

D. Renee Brecht, who serves as program director, Delaware Bayshores Program at American Littoral Society, is a Millville history buff. Here she retells the story of Luna Park, later known as Union Lake Park, now just a memory to longtime residents:

Carousel at the park was a

The Bloody Third
By: Eileen Bennett & Nelson Trout

Major attraction for children.

According to Brecht, "The Union Lake Amusement Park, later known as Luna Park, closed in 1928. Some of the sturdiest existing buildings, primarily boat houses, along with other, newer buildings, became the summer homes of several middle class families until the mid-20th century when they were replaced by the present day park and housing development known as 'Woodland Shores.'

Millville resident Kem Salvo (now a retired municipal court judge) owned a place there. "Kem recounts stories of growing up as a child on the lake and spending time at the summer cottages. They would head outside early in the morning, investigating, exploring, playing, and often not returning home until dark," Brecht said.

The popular carousel could be seen at the Entrance to Union Lake Park.

Photo courtesy of Dale Wettstein

"One year," Kem recalls, "local kids built a 25-foot bonfire at the lake, after the Millville/Vineland Thanksgiving Day football game." Standing there, marveling at the site of a bonfire of such magnitude, he heard Suzie Whitaker, whose family had a cottage Park-side, yelling.

"Hey! That's our outhouse burning on the top of a bonfire!"

And indeed, it was. In fact, all of the cottages originally had outhouses and water pumps. There was no heat or insulation. "It wasn't until the 1950s that people put in toilets and septic systems," Brecht said.

"Sometime during the 1970s when Union Lake was drained," Kem recalls, "there were a large number of bobbin spindles found near the bottom, just sitting on top of the lakebed. Through the years, they had been dumped in the lake by Millville Manufacturing." These are just some of any number of curious stories that exist about Luna Park, Union Lake, and the entire area. Millville resident Gerry Moore remembers one conversation with an old-timer who used to fish the river further downstream: "When I was young, I'd catch blue fish in these waters. Sometimes I'd catch red fish too. And other times, they'd be green. All depended on what dye they'd be using in the bleachery that day." Third-Warders got used to this, said Leon Williams. "In the sixties, myself and other kids from Middle Avenue swam at Carp Stream. Our skin was blue for about a month. The doctor said not to worry about our blue skin; it would go away…someday"

"According to Bob Francois, one Irish fellow, more often inebriated than not, would repeatedly sing a song about forty cats and forty kittens, while they chopped down trees to form the lake so many years earlier – hence, the name, "Forty Cats." The island had another name, too; one which suggested that it was the place to visit for '*au naturale*' bathing," Brecht said. That area was notoriously known as *Bare Ass Beach*."

"The summer cottages came to their demise, in the 1950s. The Maurice River Company grew out of the Millville Manufacturing Company and offered all individuals living in the cottages the opportunity to purchase their lot when Woodland Shores was proposed for development."

The Ice Box

Union Lake not only provided reprise from summer's heat, it also served to preserve food for Third Warders. In an interview in January, 2003, Brecht shared her memories of ice harvesting on Union Lake: "My grandmother, Sarah Elisabeth Sooy, remembered when refrigerators weren't refrigerators, but rather, as she would call them, 'ice boxes.' And my mother, Grace, recalls that growing up in Millville, once a week ice would be delivered for their icebox. Those who lived in town were serviced by a cart pulled by horses. Those who lived on the outskirts of town were serviced by a truck. Every week, each family would put a card in their window that would have a number on it – the number of blocks of ice that they wanted delivered that week.

"My grandfather, Edward Pangburn, worked at the ice plant for a number of years. As a child, I recall visiting the Whitaker's Ice Plant with my father and entering the cold freezers as my father would get the frozen items he had stored in his rented freezer I do remember it being so very cold, even in the middle of the summer.

Ice boating on Union Lake was a popular winter sport.

Photo courtesy of Dale Wettstein

"The source of Whitaker's Ice was local, having been harvested from Union Lake, Hankins Pond, and Silver Lake. Some people in the know say that the Burchams also harvested ice on the river as well."

Harvesting the ice from the lake was no elementary task. It required precision and skill. Brecht explained further:

"The ice was not harvested until the lake was sufficiently frozen over enough to fill the ice house, usually three times a season. Typically the ice blocks harvested on Union Lake were up to 18 inches thick. The snow, if any, was first removed and the top of the ice wet, typically by carefully drilling holes in select areas. Measuring the grids on the ice was critical to the cutting of the ice.

Once measured out, horses were used to pull a tool that would cut grooves in squares on the top of the ice. The men then followed behind and using a deeper blade, would cut deeper into the ice, but leaving the bottom of the ice intact. Using chisels, they were then separated into 'rafts' of blocks that the horses would tow to the ice house. There, the ice blocks were stored in saw dust in storage barns, known as ice houses, until they were needed."

Tragedy at the Lake

Sadly, over the years, the waters of Union Lake have claimed several young lives. According to news reports, a major tragedy occurred on April, 20, 1965. It was about 1:30 p.m. Four youngsters were three-quarters of a mile out in Union Lake when their rowboat capsized. Reportedly, they were all good swimmers. But authorities believed they must have panicked when they all fell into the lake. Only fourteen-year-old Thomas Locke was able to save himself. He was safe when taken to Millville Hospital, but suffered from shock and submersion. The body of Florence "Tootsie" Lacivita, also fourteen, was recovered. According to news reports, "efforts were under way to recover the bodies of William Barrett, fifteen, owner of the eight-foot rowboat, and fifteen-year-old Patty Reiser."

Suzy Schwegel, a lifelong resident of 200 Sharp Street in the Third Ward, knew all the youngsters who died, as did her siblings. She was at the lake the day of the tragedy. The incident was particularly jarring for the Schwegel family because of an accidental snafu by the authorities. Police were supposed to be dispatched to 200 Park Street to deliver the grim news. However, they mistakenly went to 200 Sharp Street and delivered Elsie Schwegel the horrific news instead.

"It was terrible," Suzy recalled. "My mom freaked out."

The error was soon corrected, but the trauma had been done. Afterward, the Schwegel children couldn't accept that their friends had drowned. They wandered around Union Lake for days, certain their friend would be found, and found safely. It was not to be.

Another Third Ward native, Billy Haas, also was there the day of the drowning. Refusing to believe his friend Billy Barrett was gone, Billy and some friends also searched the shoreline until young Billy Barrett's body was found.

"That was hard to take," Haas remembered recently.

McNeal Street Tragedy

On June 26, 1964, a tragedy would occur on McNeal Street so shattering, that people from the Third Ward still speak of it in whispers that continue to resonate four decades later with shock and sorrow. On that day, the now-defunct Millville Daily screamed of the tragedy in a headline befitting the declaration of World War III:

"Mother Hangs Three-Year-Old Twins in Cellar."

A sub-headline continued:

"Wakes Husband To Tell Him of Double Tragedy."

The news article story began:

'*Come at once. My wife has just hung my two babies.*' "That was the telephone message received at Millville Police headquarters shortly after ten a.m. today from fifty-year-old Alfred Riendeau of 22 W. McNeal St.," the paper reported.

"Patrolman Walter Kycynka was assigned to the call and when he arrived he found the bodies of Joan and Ann Riendeau, three-year-old twins already blue from strangulation, lying on a couch where they had been placed by their distraught father. The children had been hung," the article continued.

"Officer Kycynka, although he felt certain there was no life left in the bodies, attempted mouth to mouth resuscitation until the children could be moved by American Legion ambulance to Millville Hospital where they were pronounced dead."

The article reported that the father had just finished working the night shift at eight o'clock that morning. He watched television for a few minutes with his seven-year-old son, Mark, and the twins; then he headed to bed.

It continued, stating that,

"Still another son, Paul, age thirteen, was asleep upstairs. He woke up at ten a.m. It was about that time that Mrs. Riendeau is said to have awakened her husband to tell him she had hung the twins.

"Mr. Riendeau ran to the basement and found the two girls hanging by short pieces of clothesline from the bracing between the beams of the cellar. A third noose, which police theorize Mrs. Riendeau had fashioned for herself, was still hanging unused from the braces.

"Mrs. Riendeau, the former Emma Chambers, is 39 years old. Police say they were called once before when she injured the twins by bumping their heads against a wall. The matter was not prosecuted at the time because Mrs. Reindeau was committed to a mental institution from which she was later released.

Police said this morning that the woman had been under psychiatric treatment for some time, and that only yesterday she was an out-patient from which she was later released." The community was stunned by the sheer enormity of the tragedy.

Even today, former Third Warders recall the incident.

"I remember that so clearly," said Suzy Schwegel, who lived nearby as a child.

"It was so incredibly sad." Bill McCormick who lived for a time in the Third Ward still remembers the incident: "Tragic. Just awful."

The June 27 edition of The Millville Daily brought even more heart-breaking news. The headline screamed:

"Mother Wanted To Aid Children Because of Her Mental Problems."

The newspaper carried separate photos of the smiling, pretty twins. According to the paper, "Mrs. Riendeau was admitted to the New Jersey State Maximum Security Hospital, Trenton, late yesterday afternoon after police say she confessed to hanging her twin three-year-old daughters, Joan and Ann. Det.

Lt. Charles Pangburn said the woman confessed to hanging the children 'to help them' and that she has undergone treatment for mental illness since shortly after their birth." The paper reported that Mrs. Riendeau faced two complaints of first-degree murder. They were signed against her with warrants sent to the hospital. Further psychiatric tests were planned.

The article continued: "According to detectives, the former Emma Chambers told them she thought she was helping the girls. The officers said she has been confined in mental institutions on three occasions and that she is currently under psychiatric care. Questioning revealed that Mrs. Riendeau was committed to an institution twice, shortly after the birth of the twins. The police said the shock of their birth brought on the first mental problem."

Of course, post-partum depression was not a common term back then, and many people familiar with the story believe Mrs. Riendeau was, indeed, suffering from that. Doctors today know the symptoms to look for in regard to post-partum depression, but back in the 1960s, it isn't surprising for them to think the "shock of their birth" was the cause of the mental problem.

The newspaper reported that the "young mother was out of the state hospital for more than two years and went back again for several days about two months ago. She has been home since undergoing further psychiatric care." Whether she suffered post-partum depression after giving birth to her older children is unknown.

The true devastation of post-partum depression was shockingly clear in the June 2001 case of Andrea Yates of Texas, who drowned her five children in their bathtub. She too believed she was "saving" her children. It later was discovered that she had been suffering for some time with some very severe post-partum depression and post-partum psychosis.

But back in 1964, *postpartum depression* was not yet "discovered." The 1964 article continued:

"Police said that Mrs. Riendeau indicated that she felt her mental problems had gone over to the children and that she thought she was helping them to be 'peaceful.' She allegedly said that she thought she had caused them to be out of control.

"Police said the mother has a clear account of the hangings and that she appeared calm and apathetic during and after questioning throughout yesterday morning and afternoon.

"Lt. Pangburn, who conducted interrogations of Mrs. Riendeau and her husband, along with detectives Charles Chilakos and George Garrison, said she told them the thought to hang the children came to her while she was washing clothes.

"She told detectives she was doing the laundry in the basement when she made nooses and tied them in place between rafters. According to police, Ann was with her and that she was hung first. She then went to the yard for Joan and took her to the cellar.

"Police who arrived at her home and inspected the basement said there were no signs of a struggle. Lt. Pangburn added that there was no indication of violence and that Mrs. Riendeau told him their deaths were 'peaceful.'

She told the questioners that she was alone at the time.

"Lt. Pangburn said that the next thing Mr. Riendeau remembered was his wife awakening him and stating that she had just hung the babies. He related that he was shocked and asked her to repeat herself."

"They dashed to the basement," the paper reported. "He said he took a child in each arm and called for Mrs. Riendeau to help. Detectives stated the husband told them she came and helped get the youngsters down. They were taken upstairs and placed on a couch and police were called. According to police, Mr. Riendeau has encouraged his wife in her psychiatric treatment.

"Police arrived at the home shortly after ten o'clock and Mrs. Riendeau was taken to City Hall where she remained until late afternoon." She later was transferred to a Trenton facility.

Pat Caruso, who lived at 19 E. McNeal St., - just houses away from the Riendeaus at 22 W. McNeal St. - recalled how the entire McNeal Street neighborhood was cordoned off by Millville Police, with seemingly every member of the police force at the scene.

"The whole of McNeal Street had the neighbors standing outside, trying to find out what happened," Caruso said. "When we learned that a woman snapped, killed two of her children, I remember the crowd being devastated. Everyone was so solemn and quiet."

The following day, The Millville Daily reported the aftermath of the tragedy, stating:

"The entire community mourned the deaths of the twins, especially the first responders.

"Yesterday was a sad day for the Alfred Riendeau family with the double killing of the couple's twin daughters, Joan and Ann, both three years old. It was also a sad day for the members of the Millville Police Department and others who were called into the case in official capacities.

"According to one observer to the efforts to revive the children, no eye was dry when efforts to bring the children back to life proved futile.

"The attempts to save the lives of the twins started from the moment Patrolman Walter Kycynka and Jay Veltman arrived at the McNeal St. residence to find the children lying on a sofa in the living room of the house. The children's faces were both purplish, their arms were cold, and no pulse could be found."

The officers, according to the report, desperately continued mouth-to-mouth resuscitation until they reached the hospital in separate ambulances. At the hospital, doctors and nurses continued the frantic efforts to give life to the children but to no avail. When Coroner Benjamin Rocap arrived, the deed had been done. He pronounced the children dead from strangulation. He said the only marks on their bodies were those from the ropes that had been placed about their necks.

"When police arrived at the Riendeau home, they said the father and a son, Mark, age seven, were crying. They related that an older son, Paul, age thirteen, was more composed and that Mrs. Riendeau was at a kitchen table.

"Lt. Mulford Watson, a veteran of twenty-three years on the police force, said the incident was the first of its kind that he could remember in the city. The reaction of the rest of the police who worked on the case was pretty much that stated by one of the members. He said it was the worst experience he has had during his years on the force."

What happened to Mrs. Riendeau? Although there are no public records, many people claim she served time either in a prison or a mental hospital for a few years before being released.

Third Warder Bill McCormick said after serving some two years in a mental institute, she returned home, only to hang herself in the same basement.

There are no state records on her case. The only signs of the tragedy are graves in Mount Pleasant Cemetery. Another resident of the neighborhood, Fran Menz, who lived at 11 W. McNeal St., recalls the sad, final ending of the story with Emma's suicide.

Joan and Ann are buried in a sunny section of the 1901 cemetery, with a pink granite stone marking their birth and death dates. Nearby is a stone marked "Adelaide Emma," with the years 1925 to 1976 on it. One other stone marks Alfred's grave, with dates: "1925-1980."

House Calls

Does anyone remember when doctors made house calls? They actually would drive to your house, with their black bags and diagnosed your illness from the *comfort* of your bed. In this day and age of health insurance and long waits in emergency rooms, the idea that doctors once did that seems amazing.

Dr. Richard Beck, who now lives on Fernwood Road in the upscale area of the Third Ward, was one of those doctors. He ministered not only to Third Ward residents, but to people throughout the city. His young patients from back then, are now adults – parents and grandparents – who remember him fondly.

"Dr. Beck was great," said Cheryl Ennals. "I remember he moved into the little office on High Street, near the Foundry. He came to my house many times for my tonsillitis when I was little."

Now eighty-eight years old, Dr. Beck, an internist, is retired. After a stint in the military with a distinguished service record, Dr. Beck returned to Millville in 1955 to practice medicine. As his family grew, Dr. Beck, one of six children, said his parents moved them into larger and larger houses all over Millville (although never in the Third Ward).

"We were scattered all over," he said. "We lived in five different houses growing up. Ironically, in my practice, I made house calls in each of those houses."

He was a child of the Great Depression, something he remembers quite well. Even though his parents were not desolate, his father had to take a job in the city bleachery at the cotton mill during the Depression.

"The cotton mills were going full blast," Dr. Beck recalled. "People have no idea how bad the Depression was. We didn't have *school lunches* back then. You walked home to go to lunch. I remember walking by the soup kitchens and seeing my classmates standing in line, waiting for something to eat. You can always tell a *Depression child* because they never expected anything. They were grateful for whatever they got."

Even though Dr. Beck didn't officially live in the Third Ward, he often spent time there playing with friends. He was a member of the Boy Scout troop based at the Second Methodist Church.

"I never considered myself a 'Third Warder,' but I did spend most of my time in the Third Ward," Dr. Beck said. "Kids were much freer than they are now. Although he estimated that "50 percent" of his practice was based at Millville Hospital, the remainder of his time was spent making house calls to people all over the city. Dr. Beck brushes off any compliments about making houses calls, saying it was just "something we did."

According to Larry Haas, Dr. Beck literally saved his life in March of 1960.

"I woke up with a slight fever and a pain in my side,: Larry said. "Dr. Beck made a house call with his black leather bag and ordered blood work. Everything turned out to be in the normal range, but Dr. Beck wasn't convinced, so he ordered more tests for later in the day. Those showed an elevated white cell count and the pain in my side was worse. Later that afternoon, Dr. Alfred Davies removed my appendix. He said that if we had waited until morning, my appendix would have burst. Dr. Beck's knowledge and dedication saved me from a far more serious situation."

Suzy Schwegel of Sharp Street recalled;
"Dr. Beck was still making some house calls up to about 10 years ago. I sang for his wife's funeral at St. John Bosco (Church). I sang *Safety Harbor* for the first time. I did not know until he called me after the funeral, that he and his wife were sailors and had once sailed their own boat to Bermuda, so the song really meant something to him. Another '*God incidence.*' I stand amazed! He was a very kind and generous man."

Patti Clark Kears – who did not technically live in the Third Ward - also recalled the doctor with fondness.

"Dr. Beck was my doctor from the time he started practicing until he retired. Sometimes his bedside manner could have been adjusted, but he was a great medical doctor. My little brother went into a coma very suddenly one Sunday morning. My parents rushed him to Millville Hospital emergency room. One of the doctors diagnosed him as being abused by my parents. Anyone who knows, or knew, my parents would know that was a misdiagnosis.

"Dr. Beck strode into the room, checked him, diagnosed hypoglycemia, ordered glucose IV and transferred him to The Children's Hospital of Philadelphia."

The Schwegel family

Suzy Schwegel, sixty-nine, grew up in the Third Ward in a house at 200 Sharp Street, along with her siblings: Gregory, fifty-eight; Martin, sixty-two; Dennis, sixty-six; and another brother, Larry, who passed away years ago. Suzy still lives in the house built by her great grandfather in 1954.

The siblings – and Martin's wife Carol, who still lives with him today not far from the Sharp Street homestead – gathered recently to reminisce about their childhood, living in

Swimming lessons at Union Lake were a must!

The Third Ward. Although they were all aware of the nickname, *The Bloody Third*, they didn't see any real violence growing up. "We had everything we needed right here (in the Third Ward),"

Dennis said. "We had the lake and the ball fields; we never felt the need to leave the neighborhood."

"We walked everywhere," Suzy added. "We didn't need a car." No one locked their doors. When their mother, Elsie, wanted to summon her children home, she would ring a huge butcher's bell that could be heard for miles.

Ironically, the friction between Protestants vs. Catholics almost put a crimp in the marriage of Elsie and her husband John. "She, a Methodist, was not allowed near here in the Catholic side of town," Suzy said with a smile. Somehow the two

The eighth grade graduation from St. Mary Magdalen Church in 1962

lovebirds found a way; they were married in St. Mary's Rectory because Elsie wasn't Catholic, she couldn't be married in the church.

The Schwegel family recalls grand times in the neighborhood: When it snowed, Sharp Street was closed to traffic – partly due to safety and partly to allow children to sled down the hill. Elsie was basically a stay-at-home mom, while her husband worked on Whitaker's Ice Truck, delivering ice on a horse and buggy. "The horse was kept on Church Street," Suzy said. "In the winter, the ice was cut from Union Lake."

The Bloody Third
By: Eileen Bennett & Nelson Trout

Leon Loper and Ed Reed man Whitaker's Ice Wagon,
A common sight in the Third Ward and the rest of the city.

Photo courtesy of Dale Wettstein

Fran Menz

Fran Menz, seventy-three, was born and raised in the *Third Ward*. "My parents lived at 11 W. McNeal Street," Menz said. "They had eight children."

Fran married and moved away, but when her marriage failed, she moved back to the neighborhood, her four boys in tow. She moved to 5 W. McNeal St. – fortunately and serendipitously – next door to her parents. That came in quite handy when Fran had to work. Her parents would watch the boys.

Menz scoffed at the idea of a "bloody" Third, although she admitted she was well aware the neighborhood had a dubious reputation. Recalling her childhood, Menz said she felt safe and happy. "My parents had eight children – we lived in a house with three bedrooms and one bath. Somehow, we made it work. We were free to play outside. When the 5'o'clock whistle blew, we knew it was time to come home and eat." Menz said the Third Ward children didn't buy into the "Bloody Third" nickname. "We would hear an ambulance and we'd say, 'There goes another TWA," a reference to 'Third Ward Action,' a sarcastic nod to the nickname."

Firefighters showing off their new trucks at the Millville Fire Department No. 2 on Church Street.

Ambulance sirens weren't uncommon to the neighborhood because the hospital was nearby.

"The worst thing that ever happened was a suicide-murder right next to my mother's house," Menz said. "We heard the gunshots. Everyone on the block called 911. It was sad. When the cops got there, they had no idea what was going on. They took one of the (couple's) older boys and put him in handcuffs." That was before police realized it was a murder-suicide and the boy actually was a victim.

"That was just heart-breaking," Menz said. Her father was working at Wheaton Glass when he heard about the shootings on McNeal Street. Since one of his younger daughters often played at that address, he frantically made his way home. One can only imagine his relief when he found his children were all safe. But the neighborhood mourned the event.

"It was just awful," Menz said.

Menz treasures her childhood memories growing up on McNeal Street. But seeing it in its deteriorated state today saddens her.

"To see the destruction there; it's just terrible," she said.

Over the years, the city has tried to clean up the Third Ward, razing uninhabitable structures and known drug dens. A search in news archives finds stories of efforts of city officials to breathe life into the Third Ward. As far back as 1980, city officials undertook a major project, on McNeal Street.

Unfortunately it was mostly cosmetic – removing overgrown and rotted trees and shrubbery and fixing crumbling sidewalks. It was about this time that the city adhered to federal guidelines and made curbs handicap-accessible, also as a part of this project.

The Haas Family

Since at least the turn of the previous century, the Haas family has been a mainstay in the *Third Ward*. The family's homestead on Sharp Street, next to the canal, was always a busy place. Bill "Billy" Haas is the son of Bud Haas and the grandson of Jimmy Haas. As a young man, Bud "Mule" Haas, the South Jersey Blister, was a prize fighter, winning 47 of 48 professional boxing matches in the 1930s.

James A. Haas Sr. sleds down the Sharp Street hill in 1933. That's the bridge over the canal behind him and old Haas homestead in the background. Of particular interest is the third floor window, James's sons's bedroom at the time, overlooking the street light by the canal.

Photo courtesy of the Haas family

"In those days, for the most part, they taped up your hands. Boxing gloves were only used once in a while until they changed the rules," Bill said of his dad.

Bud Haas was a very nice man and a gentleman – until he stepped into the ring. When he won, he could make as much as a hundred dollars. That was a: lot of money back then. He later settled into a *regular* job, raising Billy and Billy's older brother, Buddy.

Buddy Haas was a big kid, standing at least 6'3" and weighing in at well over 250 pounds. Buddy was a mild-mannered, fun-loving person and a terrific football player for

Millville Senior High School. Sadly, Buddy passed away a few years ago.

Living right next to the canal, the Haas boys and the rest of the neighborhood kids would swim there in the summer. There was a rope tied to a tree and they would swing out and let go, splashing and laughing. They also hiked around the Union Lake Bluffs, from the first cove to the third.

"We knew every bush and tree up there at the bluffs. What a cool place to play and hang out!"

Millville City Park, a little down river from the Third Ward, was also a spot where the Third Ward kids would go to play. Often they would meet up with some kids from the west side of town. On many more than one occasion, fist fights would break out between the two groups. The *Third Ward* boys would usually win. They were a good-hearted bunch of youngsters, but mostly feared by those in other sections of town.

According to Dr. Christopher Haas, an interventional cardiologist who lives in Cape May County, there is a Haas family legend regarding the Third Ward.

"My grandfather and his brothers were all born in the first house on the right, just over the Sharp street canal heading away from Main Street. I believe it was 527 Sharp," he said. "In the early to mid-1920's my grandfather, Lawrence Haas, was somewhat sickly, so in order to entertain him, his brothers, Dick and Bud, would arrange prize fights in the street under a lamppost. It is said the opponents were almost always the Polish immigrants from the area. My grandfather would watch the fights from his bedroom window.

"Legend has it that the Haas boys never lost a fight, and most of the opponents essentially needed to be scraped up off the road. These were not street brawls per se, but rather organized matches with rounds etc. I don't know if they wore gloves. In any case, I wonder if this had any hand in the Third Ward gaining its moniker *The Bloody Third*."

Bill McCormick and Pals

Bill McCormick lived at 18 McNeal St. from the age of four until just after his twelfth birthday, from 1951-1959. His memories are clear, happy, mostly heartwarming, and sometimes, heart-breaking. He remembers the coal heater in the basement which never kept the house much above freezing on the coldest of winter days. He recalls how he and his brothers would jockey for a seat on the kitchen floor above the only air vent in the house.

But McCormick, today a successful business owner, said: "Hey, looking back, they were magical times. We were pretty close to being poor. It was before my father worked his way up to plant manager at Wheaton Glass. He didn't make a lot of money then. Everybody in the *Third Ward* was in the same boat. I wouldn't change a thing. I had a good family and a lot of good friends. We had nothing, but didn't miss anything!"

*Bill McCormick and his dad
"Bud" share a quiet moment.*

Photo courtesy of the McCormick family.

McCormick's best friend in those days was Jack Walker, who now owns a car dealership in the neighboring city of Vineland. When he is back in town, Bill stops in to see Jack and reminisce about their days growing up on the hard streets of the

Bloody Third Ward. They talk with great fondness about people like Phil Richter, Hank Fein and Butch Barbose.

"All of us guys played sports. Hank Fein and Butch Barbose were awesome athletes. So were Bill McCormick and his little brother Jimmy, who most people in Millville still refer to as *The Legend,* as his prowess and strength on the football field was so great."

McCormick smiled.

"I'm really proud of Jimmy," he said. "The whole town is proud of him."

Madeleine Demillio and Bernadette Thompson are a couple of the girls in the neighborhood that visit McCormick's memories today. Most of his friends went to St. Mary Magdalen School, which was a few blocks away from 18 McNeal Street. "We always walked to school. In those days your parents never drove you to school.

"There was an older kid named Tony Martin who always used to bully us younger boys. I used to get sick to my stomach just thinking about seeing him on the way to school. For three of four years, there was a row of hedges in one of the yards. I used to hide behind them just to stay out of Tony's way."

Bill McCormick eventually grew to be 6'4" and over 225 pounds, becoming an all-around athlete at Millville Senior High School. He later graduated from Villanova University. One of Bill's best friends, with whom he roomed at Villanova, is the screenwriter and actor Leo Rossi.

McCormick remembers a girl named "Pinky" who was very attractive. She used to turn the boys' heads with her tight, provocative clothing.

"That was when we were just starting to notice girls. Surprisingly," McCormick said, "Pinky became a nun, and after that career, had a sex change operation and is now a man. That was a real shocker."

When McCormick was growing up, the family had a telephone with no dial that could only get four numbers: Three family members and one close friend. "We had to go through the operator to make phone calls."

There were good times and bad in that era of McCormick's life. He happily remembered his Uncle Leon Horin and Bobby Taylor coming over to play catch out in the yard. McCormick looked back to the 1960s when he and his buddies would play in the woods before Arlene Village, an apartment complex in the Third Ward, was built. The complex reportedly was named after the owner's daughter.

"They tore our woods down to build Arlene Village. Before that, it was really a nice piece of woods with a stream running through it. We used to catch turtles, lizards, frogs and snakes over there. Good memories. Good times. There were fist fights," he said, "sometimes bloody, but, we always made up a day or two later."

Flipping baseball cards was something else the nitty-gritty boys of the *Third Ward* would do for fun. They would also bend now-valuable baseball cards so they would zing against the spokes of their bicycles, making the bikes sound like they had an engine.

Haas said when they weren't playing in the streets or up at the bluffs, and had a little money, there were a couple of stores in which to hang out.

"Goldie's" was located at the corner of Broad and Dock streets. Goldie's either had moved, or was about to move to that location from 222 McNeal St. The gang could get sodas, candy and sandwiches there. They also played the pin-ball machine and shot pool at "Goldie's.

On the northeast corner of Foundry and McNeal streets, "Lacivita's" was another favorite spot. "There were always a bunch of Fonzie wannabes hangin' out in there, long before Fonzie ever hit television on Happy Days," Haas said with a laugh. "Pool was the big attraction at Lacivita's. The owner took it so seriously that one day when there wasn't enough room for him to make a tight shot and his cue stick was cramped against the wall, he went into the back room. A couple of minutes later he came out with a jig-saw and cut a hole in the wall." Another part of the same building was used as a beauty salon.

Riding around in his pick-up truck, Haas treated this author to various locations around the *Third Ward* pointing out numerous landmarks, explaining how things have changed since the fifties and sixties.

"At 645 Buck Street," he said, there used to be Charlie DeToro's barber shop. He used to cut our hair there for almost nothing. He knew that most of us kids didn't have much, so I guess that was his way of *helping out.*" An old man named Billy Fallows used to raise parakeets in his back yard at 221 McNeal Street. "Mr. Fallows always had a cigarette in his mouth. He'd take the birds inside during cold weather to keep them warm."

Jim McFadden who lived at 215 Foundry Street was the first male gymnast to ever complete what is called *"The Giant Swing,"* a difficult maneuver even today in the world of men's gymnastics.

"There was a little park on Foundry Street with steel monkey bars. We made up a game called *"hang and tag."* Everybody would hang from a rung on the bars except for *"the puller." The puller* would try to yank the *hangers* away from their grip on the bars. The *hangers* could kick the *puller* in the face; and we did. The last one left on the bars won the game and could choose the next *puller."* Haas said. "We created our own fun in the *Third Ward.*

"There were a couple of slightly older guys who used to set up fist fights for the younger boys. Ronnie Reeves and George Reiser did this for their own amusement. The fights took place in an alley behind the 800 block of Archer Street.

When word got around that you were supposed to fight that day or night, you'd better be there. If you didn't show up, Ronnie and George would hunt you down and beat you up real good. So we always showed up even if we had to fight our best friend. It's just how things were back in the *Third Ward* in those days," McCormick recalled. "We thought it was like that everywhere. I guess it wasn't, though. For some reason, it was called 'Tade Alley.' It's where most of us smoked our first cigarette. From then on us guys in the Third used to call cigarettes *'tades'.*"

Haas remembers with great fondness his days growing up in *The Bloody Third Ward* with friends like Vaughn Stites, the Reiser brothers, Garry, Hemmy and Gilbert Cheeseman, George and Eddie Reiser, Bob Jones, the Lahendro boys, Earl and Billy Barrett, Joe Carty, Huey Parr, Doug Langley and Andy Dessario.

"Yep, I remember them all. We used to ride our bikes down this real steep gravel hill up at the top of first cove. We called it *'Suicide Hill,'* because most of the time you either crashed your bike or ended up in the lake. I guess that kind of sums up what it was like growing up in the *Third Ward* in the fifties and sixties. We took a lot of chances, but we had a lot of fun. We learned about life the hard way."

McCormick reflected that, "My days of growing up in the Third Ward are priceless. They were hard times, but they were great times. I'm really glad I grew up there, even though some of those years were far from easy."

"High Jinks"

In October 1930, most everybody in Millville as well as the rest of South Jersey had their attention focused on the sky above the Levoy Theater on High Street in the Holly City. Harry *Had* Elliot was perched on the top of a flagpole there.

Crowds gathered to watch Harry "Had" Elliott sitting on a flagpole outside the Levoy Theater. He broke the record by sitting atop the pole for 51 days and six hours.

The flamboyant Elliot had climbed up the flagpole on September 11, and would remain there for several weeks.

Elliot, who was also a boxer and had fought in the ring at Union Lake Park, was quite a character. Bill McCormick recalls his father telling the tale of the man on the pole.

"From what I heard from my dad, Elliot was somewhat of an adventurer too, and a legend in the *Third Ward*. Dad said that Millville had a lot of neat people back then, and that Millville was like no other place in the world. The flagpole thing must have been awesome. Dad used to tell us all about it."

An armchair was attached to the top of the flagpole and Elliot was attended to by a manager and an official ground crew. An electric light was even set up so that the scores of spectators and fans could observe Elliot both day and night. Letters of encouragement were sent to Elliot from all over. He got an invitation from the seaside resort of Wildwood, New Jersey to sit atop a flagpole at the ocean's edge, which would undoubtedly attract even more vacationers to the city. Elliot graciously turned down the invitation.

Elliot was bound and determined to break the flagpole sitting world record, which at the time was fifty days. "Shipwreck" Kelly had spent fifty days above Atlantic City's Steel Pier earlier in the summer of 1930.

While Elliot was in his temporary armchair home, members of the Millville Fire Department were nearby, helping to make his stay as comfortable as possible. They did this without breaking the "rules of flagpole sitting." They could not touch him in any way, nor could the firemen assist him in his quest for the world record, such as propping him up or reinforcing his situation in any physical manner after he was originally settled into his legendary armchair in the sky. "They just kind of kept an eye on him to make sure he didn't pass out or start to fall," McCormick remembers his dad saying of the firemen.

The 1915 American LaFrance Hose Wagon on Church Street.

Photo courtesy of Dale Wettstein

Elliot had to deal with insects, thunder and lightning storms and cold nights. He wrapped himself in blankets and heavy coats and pants when he had to. People, some of whom were on the roof of the Levoy, said Elliot was "almost like a contortionist." He would twist and turn, dressing and undressing, determined to break the record of fifty days.

During his six weeks on the flagpole, the Handy Restaurant provided him three meals a day. Other Millville residents sent up toothpaste and a toothbrush along with fruit and cigarettes. As time went on, Elliot seemed almost surreal to those who gazed upon him during the day and eerily illuminated by night, *Had* Elliot had become an almost unbelievable attraction – a quirky legend in his own time and a unique kind of hero.

With a scraggly beard, tired and shaky legs and a world record under his belt, Elliot climbed down from his flagpole after fifty-one days and six hours. To this day, *Had* Elliot remains one of the most colorful and accomplished characters of all time, not only in the *Third Ward*, but in all of Millville history.

"Sure wish I could have been around for that. I'm glad my dad was. I always loved hearing that story," McCormick said.

The great Opera House fire at High and Sassafras streets, unknown date.
Many Third-Warders enjoyed shows and entertainment here.

Photo courtesy of Dale Wettstein

The 1917 Porreco Massacre

Many old-timers firmly believe it was an infamous December 1917 massacre that sparked the name *"Bloody Third."* Perhaps that's because the Porreco crime was so heinous. There's no doubt it was one of the most notorious incidents in the *"Bloody Third."* News accounts referred to the carnage as the "most horrible crime which has been committed in South Jersey for many years."

The ironic part of this item is that it has been handed down through the decades in my husband, Chick Bennett's, family. Chick's grandmother Lareine Landell Bennett, in 1917, was a young housewife of 21 when she witnessed part of this tragedy. Lareine lived at 318 W. Green St., but was visiting relatives at 402 W. Powell St. That freak moment in time would give Chick's grandmother a front-row ticket to the bloodbath.

"My grandmother told us this story over the years," Chick said. "She said she was standing on the front porch of 402 W. Powell St. when she saw a man scurry into the outhouse, pursued by an army of police officers, all the time shots ringing through the air."

The story is being told here as it was reported, verbatim, in the now-defunct *The Bridgeton Evening News*. Because newspaper reporters had a much more dramatic writing license than today, we believe the original account is much more riveting than a mere retelling of events. This article appeared in the Dec. 13, 1917 edition of *The Bridgeton Evening News*:

"James Porreco Shot Entire De Luca, Family at Their Home On West Broad Street Last Night; Daughter Escaped by Leaping Through Window – The Murderer Escaped.

"Brooding over fancied wrongs, James Porreco, who lived apart from his family, invaded their home, 126 West Broad street, last evening, and murdered four people. He escaped and the police searched the locality without finding any trace of him.

"The dead are; Benjamin De Luca, aged 38 years. 126 Broad street; Mrs. Columbo De Luca, his wife, aged 28 years. Same address; Sarah, aged 6 years, daughter of Mr. and Mrs. De Luca; Mrs. Mary Porreco, aged 49 years, 126 Broad street."

"Belle Porreco, aged 17 years, is in the Millville Hospital suffering from lacerations about the arms, sustained when she leaped through a window to elude her pursuing parent.

"The other members of the Porreco family, all sons, Thomas, Louis, Dominick and Donato, were at work in the T.C. Wheaton glass factory when their father attempted to wipe out two families.

"The bodies were taken care of by Undertaker Frank Dalton, after Coroner Allison Kruse, of Vineland, had viewed them all.

The Shooting

"Belle recited the frightful tale as best she could as she lay upon a bed in the Millville Hospital last evening. Here it is:

"The Porreco family, consisting of Mrs. Porreco and five children, together with Mr. and Mrs. De Luca and their little girl, lived in the rear of the building at 126 West Broad street. Her father lived on Buck street having left his family members some months ago.

"Last evening, Belle and Mr. and Mrs. De Luca were talking when there was a knock at the side door. Mr. De Luca opened the door; and Porreco, wild-eyed and waving a double-barreled shot gun, leaped into the room. Putting the gun to his shoulder, he fired at De Luca's retreating figure; and De Luca fell dead, the discharge of shot piercing his head. Turning the gun on his wife, Mrs. Porreco, he discharged the other barrel, the shot taking effect in her head. Porreco then went out doors, probably to reload his gun.

"Belle ran upstairs, telling Mrs. De Luca to lock the door; but the latter determined to save her child, ran back shouting, "Where's my child?" Belle heard two shots; it is probable that one killed Mrs. De Luca, the charge lodging in her right side, near the kidney. It tore away part of her right arm.

"The other struck the child in the side.

The Bloody Third
By: Eileen Bennett & Nelson Trout

"The bodies of mother and daughter were found in a heap in the stairway, the child having fallen across the mother. Mrs. De Luca was soon to have become the mother of another child.

"The body of Mr. De Luca was found stretched upon the floor near the door, and that of Mrs. Porreco had fallen against the stove.

Daughter Escaped

"Porreco's daughter, Belle, leaped through an upstairs window out upon the rear shed and crashed through another window into the Lessero home.

"As she fled upstairs, the father had shot once at her. Her screams aroused the neighborhood. As she broke into the Lessero dwelling, she fell upon the floor into a faint.

"The shooting and cries of murder alarmed the locality, and within a few minutes there was a crowd upon the spot.

"Nobody saw Porreco flee. Not anybody appears to know how he left the house, although there is a story that someone said he heard someone else say that he came out of the side door and ran across the open lot.

"The shot gun and a revolver with which the shooting was done were left in the house and are in possession of the police. He also left his overcoat on an upstairs bed.

Origin of Trouble

"According to the stories that are told by Belle Porreco and others of the same family, the father and the mother were married in Italy, and all their children were born there. Thomas came to America seven years ago, and three years later was followed by the rest of the family. They have resided on Broad street only a few months, formerly having lived on Dock street. It is claimed that the father, who is about 50 years old, was shiftless and wouldn't work. Six months ago he took $600, the savings of the family, and went to Philadelphia and squandered most of the money. He became angry because his daughter Belle was friendly to Tony Torell, a clean cut young man of 103 Foundry Street. His attempts to break up the matter were frowned upon by other members of the family, and enraged because it was appropriate that the pair would wed as soon as the daughter reached her 18th birthday (she is seventeen now) he left his family and has since been living on Buck street and working at living in the Millville Traction Company's section gang.

"He has frequently made threats that he would kill his daughter, as well as other members of the family. He has told them that it would be a poor Christmas for them.

"Chris Lessero, who lives next door to the Porrecos, says that for a number of nights past, Porreco has been sneaking through his yard and peering into the Porreco windows. In an effort to prevent it, Lessero tied his dog near the gate, and Porreco came to him about it, making complain and tell him that it would be a poor Christmas in the house next door.

"The other day in the barber shop of Joe Lessero on High street, he told of the intention to purchase some shell, to which Joe asked if he was going gaming.

"Indications and evidence show that the man had threatened to kill them on innumerable occasions.

Shot at Torrell

"Last evening, Porreco visited the locality in which Tony Torrell lives and met the youth as he was returning home after being shaved at a barber shop.

"Porreco opened fire on the young man who fled down town. He says there were five shots fired at him. He doesn't know whether they came from the gun of the revolver. He hurried to City Hall, but met Officers Jesse Cossaboom and Thomas Breeden on their way to the scene of the murder, they have been informed of the tragedy over the telephone.

"Joseph Ryan, Walter Hankins and Benjamin Madkiff saw Porreco hurrying down Church Street with a gun. He was running slowly. They followed him and saw him to the Broad street house. The boys stood at the Beckett grocery store, fearing to go nearer and heard the shots fired that snuffed out four lives. They then ran to the Cotton Mill and telephoned for City Hall.

"Dr. Robert McHenry and Policemen Breeden and Cossaboom entered the house at about the same time. Life was extinct in all four bodies.

"Miss Porreco was then removed to the hospital, where Dr. McHenry attended her injuries.

"By that time, the entire police force had assembled at the Porreco home, as well as a crowd of people.

"Telephone messages were sent to the police in nearby cities to be on the lookout for the murderer.

"Porreco is a man of about 50 years of age, about 5 feet, 3 inches tall, weighing possibly 140 pounds. His face is speckled with small-pox scars. He has been wearing a small sandy mustache, but it is said that he has shaved it off within the past two days. His face is rather dark, his eyes small, the top of his head bald with the exception of a few straggling hairs. He always wears a cap and had a dark suit on last evening.

"It is said that Porreco's rage against the De Lucas was caused by his belief that they advised his wife and children what to do.

Police on Job

"Director Samuel Bennett and the entire Millville police force went to work on the case immediately. Detective Frank Lore of Bridgeton was summoned at a conference that was held in the Millville City Hall.

"It was learned that Porreco has a very close friend at Newfield and Haines; Biggs and Phifer went there in an endeavor to see what they could learn. Breeden and Lore went in another direction. The man's chances of getting out of the State are poor, telephone information having been given the police of Camden and Penn grove to prevent crossing the ferry.

"There is a theory that he probably will end his own life or has already done so, and that only his dead body will be found.

"Tony Torrell did not go to his home last night. He decided to take no changes being shot and slept in the City Hall. He will be anxious until the fellow is apprehended.

"Before his departure last evening Coroner Allison Kruse instructed Policeman Cossaboom to get him a six-man jury for an inquest, which will be held this afternoon."

The Bloody Third
By: Eileen Bennett & Nelson Trout

The following article details the next chapter of the tragedy, in the multi-headlined style of the time: \

"The Bridgeton Evening News, Thursday, Dec. 13, 1917: MURDERER DIED JUST BEFORE NOON: TODAY IN MILLVILLE HOSPITAL: POLICE CAPTURE MURDERER AFER LIVELY PISTOL DUEL:James Porreco Comes From Concealment in Edward Wallace's Barn is Discovered: Took Refuge in Outhouse on Church Street – Body was riddled with bullets: Refused to Surrender – Was Taken to Millville Hospital."

"12 O'Clock, noon – Porreco, the Italian immigrant who murdered four persons, died just before noon today in the Millville Hospital: (From Our Millville Office)

"James Porreco, slayer of his wife and Mr. and Mrs. Benjamin De Luca and their six-year-old daughter, Sarah, was captured last night shortly before 10 o'clock.

"The following was cornered in an outhouse on the property of Richard Carey, corner Church and Powell streets, and when he refused to surrender, the police opened fire. The pistol duel continued ten minutes, during which his anatomy was perforated with lead pellets."

(*This is the incident Chick's grandmother, Lareine Landell Bennett,*  *witnessed while standing on the Powell Street porch.*) "When the police brought the Italian out, a crowd of several hundred people pushed and jammed their way forward with cries of:

"Lynch him! Lynch him!"
and similar other demands. The police were obliged to draw their revolvers to keep the mob

Lareine Landell Bennett from becoming violent. After his removal to Millville Hospital, there appeared little hope for his recovery.

"Doctors C.S. Franckle, Samuel Bennett and F. Vernon Ware operated on him and bits of lead were removed from various parts of his body. There were two, one from a 32 caliber and the other a steel jacketed bullet, pierced the fellow's arm, and it was necessary to amputate the member. A couple shots entered the lower part of the abdomen and couple more to the leg.

60

"After the operation, Porreco appeared to improve and early morning was still living."

Day in the Hay

"Porreco was discovered in the barn of Edward Wallace by Edward Wallace Jr. at about half past eight o'clock last night. Ed was going to feed the horses and bumped right into the Italian. "Hello Jim," he said, but Jim wasn't feeling like talking, and he dashed out of the door and through the yard to the lane. At either end of the lane were special policemen placed there to watch the barn by Director Bennett: Jack Robinson, Harry Cossaboom, Grover Wolverton, Benjamin Wade, together with Officers Harr Phifer and Jess Cossaboom. This array of guard was not sufficient to daunt Porreco and before any of them could nab him, he had scrambled over the fence and raced through a yard to Buck street. Wade and Wolverton pursued the fleeing Italian along Buck street to Powell and into Church. He ran around back of Diligence Hall and was lost for the time.

"The alarm was broadcasted speedily, and within a few minutes, policemen Richard Haines, Carl Stratton, Thomas Breed and Charles Sharp and William Creech of the Vineland department who were in Millville, conferring with the local officers reached the scene.

"Haines discovered Porreco's footprints in the snow and saw that they led to the small building. Mrs. Giberson, who lives across the street, has said that she had seen a man run back of Carey's. Haines tried the door of the building and found it locked. The blue coats surrounded the place and called to Porreco to open the door and come out. There was no sound. The police opened fire, shooting through the door and Porreco replied. Bullets whistled through the air in a way that made the crowd scurry for shelter. A couple whizzed between Breeden and Haines, lodging in a post a foot to one side. Sharp and Haines had automatic revolvers and they emptied them in quick time. Breeden Fired till his supply of cartridges gave out, and Haines then used a shotgun. Stratton emptied his revolver. Citizens who had joined in the case shot in the building which was perforated on every side.

Shot For Ten Minutes

"The shooting continued for ten minutes. A groan was heard and feeling that the man had been wounded, Haines crept up and pried the door open. A flash of the light revealed the Italian stretched upon the floor. Breeden, Haines and Sharp went in, and brought him out. Porreco was able to walk in spite of his numerous wounds.

"Then it was that the crowd, many of them Italians, wanted to lynch him, but the police pushed their way through the throng, placed their man in an automobile and brought him to the city hall. From there he was removed to the hospital.

"Porreco displayed a great amount of nerve all the time. He talked and admitted in an ante mortem statement, that he killed his wife and Mr. and Mrs. De Luca and their little girl.

"Now get me Doc," he said. "Belly hurts. Get Doc. Fix up. Then I tell more."

"An investigation that covered all of South Jersey was conducted Tuesday night and yesterday. Haines went to Camden yesterday and watched the ferries with Biggs on the Philadelphia side. Lore and Breeden chased down half a dozen clues. Cossaboom, Stratton, Sharp and Creech went to Rosenhayn on a clue, in fact the police were leaving nothing undone in an effort to capture the murderer. From the time of the tragedy until the arrest, they were continually on the go.

"In Camden yesterday Officer Richard Haines learned from a person well acquainted with Porreco that he served a fourteen years sentence in Italy for killing a man. He has also been before a local judge of the peace on a complaint of his wife. When captured, he had $154 in his pockets and a plentiful supply of cartridges."

"On Dec. 14, 1917 the paper screamed: "PORRECO DIED CURSING ILL LUCK, DAUGHTER AT BEDSIDE. Enraged Because He Had Failed to Kill Her and Tony Torrell, Her Lover. Funerals of Four Victims Held This Morning. Jury Drawn for Coroner's Inquest."

"In the death of James Porreco, which occurred in Millville Hospital shortly before noon yesterday, as briefly told in yesterday's Evening News, retribution was meted out to the fiendish perpetrator of the most horrible crime which has committed in South Jersey for many years.

"The Italian died cursing his 17-year-old daughter who was brought to his bedside in the hope that he might at least pass into Eternity seeking God's forgiveness for his heinous deed, but Porreco retained the insane anger which has gripped him for the past week to the end, and gasps he cried out that he meant to kill her. His hate could not be satisfied, and as he struggling between life and death, he demanded that his eldest son finish the work which he had started – that he kill Tony Torrell, the young man whom the daughter, Belle, is engaged to marry.

"His body was removed to the undertaking establishment of Frank Dalton.

"This morning the funerals of the four victims, Mrs. Mary Porreco, Benjamin De Luca, Mrs. Columbo De Luca and their six-year-old daughter Sarah were held.

"For the remaining children of the Porreco family it was a trying ordeal. The service was conducted by the Rev. Joseph A. Ryan of St. Mary's Church, interment being made in Mount Pleasant Cemetery.

On Saturday, Dec. 15, 1917, The Bridgeton Evening News reported that a "Coroner's Jury Exonerates Police.' Officials, upon examining all the evidence and 11 witnesses, ruled that the police fired in self-defense. The jury consisted of six men. They deliberated for three-quarters of an hour before rendering their verdict of not guilty on all counts. Even though the verdict was a mere formality, the hearing was not without drama.

The Bridgeton Evening News reported that "Belle Porreco was the principal witness in the first case. "She was heavily veiled and was a good witness in spite of her great grief. She told the story of how her father entered the house, shot Benjamin de Luca, then aimed the gun at her mother and fired. She saw them both fall to the floor. Her father caught his toe in the carpet and stumbled, and before he could regain his balance she ran upstairs screaming to Mr. De Luca that her father was shooting at everybody in the house. She called to Mrs. De Luca to lock the stair door but the woman, thinking only of her child who was downstairs, hurried down. Belle said she heard two shots as she jumped out of the downstairs window."

House where the shootings took place.

Photo courtesy of Charles C. Bennett

Of course, there were other crimes in the *Bloody Third*, but it was the Porreco murders that seem to have been the source of the nickname "*Bloody Third.*" Several longtime residents have relatives who know of the Porreco crime and still talk about it to this day.

My husband Chick recalls his paternal grandmother retelling the

story of the outhouse horror she witnessed to her grandchildren. Until recently, when Chick saw the 1917 newspaper account, he was somewhat dubious of his grandmother's tale. Now, he's a believer. He remembered his grandmother quietly telling her young grandchildren about the *Horrible Thing* she witnessed as a fresh new bride.

Lareine Landell Bennett, the Grandmother of Chick Bennett, passed the story down to him.

Photo courtesy of Charles C. Bennett

Chick recalls listening in rapt attention to her story when he was a young boy;

"I lived on Green and Church streets, but I was visiting my family on Powell Street. "I was just a young lady – couldn't have been more than 21 – Just married. Our family was getting ready for Christmas."

His grandmother recalled that she went outside to get some air on the front porch. *"The night was still and quiet, with the smell of snow in the air,"* she said, when she heard what she first thought were firecrackers, but later proved to be the gunfire exchange between police and Porreco.

Lareine's story of "the outhouse shooting" was handed down through the generations, mostly as myth. It wasn't until recently – when the newspaper accounts of the 1917 massacre were discovered – that Chick saw his grandmother's story proven in black and white. In fact, Chick's grandmother would later testify at a coroner's inquest into the massacre.

Lareine Landell Bennett was standing on the front porch, left, here at 402 Powell Street when she saw the infamous Porreco shootout with police.

Photo courtesy of Charles C. Bennett

According to the article in the Bridgeton Evening News, Belle was the star witness at the inquest. Just days after she was released from Millville Hospital, the young woman testified against her father. "She was heavily veiled," the article stated, "and was a good witness in spite of her great grief. She told the story of how her father entered the house, shot Benjamin DeLuca, then aimed the gun at her mother and fired. She saw them both fall to the floor. Her father caught his toe in the carpet and stumbled; and before he could regain his balance she ran upstairs screaming to Mrs. DeLuca that her father was shooting at everybody in the house. She called to Mrs. DeLuca to lock the stair door but the woman, thinking only of her child who was downstairs hurried down. Belle said she heard two shots as she jumped out of the window. "Thomas Porreco, her brother, recited a long tale of the manner in which his father had acted, going back some months ago, telling of the trip to Philadelphia, when he took the family savings of $600 and of his threats lately to kill the several members of the household.

"Mrs. Rena Bennett, (Chick's grandmother, Lareine Landell Bennett) who lives next to the Porrecos, testified that she heard the gun reports and saw Porreco come out of the house. James Munsey, Lareine's brother, also saw him leave the house."

According to Maryjane Lloyd Moats:

"I am an old Third Warder. I lived on Green Street and Church Street. I had heard that a family was murdered there."

Memories differ for people who subsequently lived either at the Church Street address or nearby. Solid facts are tarnished with time. Since street numbers have changed over the years, the *"murder house"* – once listed at 126 W. Broad St. – now is considered Church and Broad streets (actually 601 Church St.)

Various news accounts verify that after shooting his victims, Porreco fled to the outhouse at Church and Powell streets. They also verify that it was there that Porreco was shot and captured.

Just days after she was released from Millville Hospital, the young Belle Porreco testified at a coroner's inquest of the murders

According to a news article in the Dec. 15, 1917 edition of *The Bridgeton Evening News*, (referred to earlier), Belle was the star witness. "She was heavily veiled," the article stated, "and was a good witness in spite of her great grief. She told the story of how her father entered the house, shot Benjamin DeLuca, then aimed the gun at her mother and fired. She saw them both fall to the floor. Her father caught his toe in the carpet and stumbled and before he could regain his balance she ran upstairs screaming to Mrs. DeLuca that her father was shooting at everybody in the house. She called to Mrs. DeLuca to lock the stair door but the woman, thinking only of her child who was downstairs hurried down. Belle said she heard two shots as she jumped out of the window.

"Thomas Porreco, her brother, recited a long tale of the manner in which his father had acted, going back some months ago, telling of the trip to Philadelphia, when he took the family savings of $600 and of his threats lately to kill the several members of the household.

"Mrs. Rena Bennett, (Chick's grandmother, Lereine Landell Bennett) who lives next to the Porrecos, testified that she heard the gun reports and saw Porreco come out of the house. James Munsey (Lereine's brother) also saw him leave the house." Not surprisingly, the police officers were exonerated of all blame.

According to Maggie Marshall Benevento, her father Dick Marshall, was born and raised on Buck Street. His father recalled the Porreco murders. Benevento said: "Rumors had it he (Porreco) hid in Whitaker's Ice Plant Hay Barn with horses overnight. The next day the police cornered him at the old fire hall on Church Street. He was cornered in an outhouse and the police and others riddled the outhouse with bullets."

Kurt M. Warner said when this family moved into the Church Street house, they heard a story that people were shot on the roof. "My father said there was still blood stains in the attic in 1956 when my father, mother and older sister moved in," he wrote. "(The) attic always gave my sisters and I the creeps."

Lois Hider, who turned 80 in September, said she lived at 601 Church Street, when she was a young girl. She vividly remembers her parents talking about the Porreco murders on Broad Street. "I lived in that house from 12 years old on until I married," said Hider, who still lives in Millville. (Church and Broad intersect, and each has a front door, so the addresses can be confusing.)

"I remember the story of the murder   .. my parents telling me that a man came bursting through the front door (on W. Broad Street). He went past someone near the stove, shot at them. A woman with a child ran up the steps. He shot both the woman and girl." It was then that the man – identified as Porreco – fled to the outhouse on Church Street, and was apprehended by police following a shootout. H`ider said she never felt uncomfortable in the Church Street house, although she admits when her parents went out for the evening, she felt "a little nervous." The stairway, where it is believed the woman and her child were shot, had no light switch, so Hider said climbing the infamous stairs to bed "was a bit spooky." The infamous outhouse remained in the back years for several more years.

Linda Morgan also lived in the infamous house at 601 Church St. "It was the murder house from the early 1900s," she said. "The man killed his whole family. My bedroom was in the second floor back room. He then crawled out of the window to the roof. And then they had a shootout on the roof!"

The infamous Church Street house where the
Porreco shootout with police took place

Photo courtesy of Charles C. Bennett

Many people questioned whether the "Porreco" name was changed to the prominent Millville name "Porreca," because of the murders. We asked Millville City Commissioner Lynne Porreca Compari and she simply said, "My parents never told me anything about that."

The 1918 Flu Pandemic

The great flu pandemic, which swept through the country, killing millions of people, across the globe, did not spare the *Third Ward*, or, indeed, any part of Millville. According to a 1918 article in *The Bridgeton Evening News*:

"Policeman Carl Stratton's condition yesterday afternoon became serious. Last evening he was delirious and it was feared that he might not survive the night. He was stricken with influenza a week ago early in the week." There followed a "stop-the-presses" bulletin: "Later, Carl Stratton died last night."

On Oct. 9, 1918, the flu epidemic was so severe in Millville, that "the industrial plants are only operating at about one-half capacity," according to an article in *The Bridgeton Evening News*. The flu had taken its toll on Third Ward workers in the plants and mills.

"The illness of several Millville physicians has made conditions worse, probably, than they otherwise would have been. In some cases entire families are down with the disease." On one day alone, the paper reported three people died, and there were a hundred cases of the flu throughout Millville, "some of them being critical." The paper declared in a headline:

"The Epidemic Seems to Have Reached Its Height."

Indeed, the paper was filled with the names of those stricken by the flu. The epidemic so ravaged the entire city, that the New Jersey Health Board banned public funerals. Tragically, survivors of the flu epidemic weren't even allowed to review the remains of their deceased loved ones – even if they were in their own home.

The flu swept through the entire county like a tsunami. Although it targeted the young and infirmed, no one was truly exempt from acquiring the deadly flu. The paper reported: "Miss Mable Johnson was taken down with influenza at her home, 417

Smith street, on Saturday night. Her two sisters are ill with the disease and her mother is also confined to her bed."

"Physicians are doing their best to care for all who need attention," the paper reported, "but the days are too short. Local drug stores are filled from early morning till late at night with a steady flow of customers, many of them being persons who are seeking preventative instead of a cure.

"In order to provide care and treatment for such cases the Millville Hospital has thrown its doors open, and the usual admission requirements will be waived during the epidemic. Every effort will be done to relieve the present condition." Some samples of cases in Millville included:

"Miss Edith Harris of East Main Street was in a very critical condition last evening. She is suffering from pneumonia."

"Edward Branin of Maurice Street is very ill with pneumonia. His condition was low last evening."

Newspapers were scrambling to keep up with reporting the latest death tolls. In the Oct. 21, 1918 edition of *The Bridgeton Evening News*, it was reported that the death toll of Millvillians during the 48-hour period terminating at midnight totaled 14 deaths from pneumonia from the disease last Saturday and Sunday." Even church services were postponed, and one pastor urged "secret devotions" by families in his congregation.

"We are trusting, however, that our churches will be open again very soon and that normal conditions will be restored," said Pastor Williamson.

The health-care givers – who were on the front lines during the pandemic – were easy victims. The paper reported that "Dr. W.P. Rickert of East Main Street, who has been critically ill with influenza, is getting along in an encouraging manner." The flu would continue to claim victims until it ran its course in 1920. If you visit any old cemetery in New Jersey, you're likely to find the dates, 1918, 1919, or 1920 on graves of children who were claimed by the flu. All told, the flu epidemic infected 50 to 100 million people worldwide, making it one of the worst disasters in human history.

Burying the Dead

The flu epidemic, sadly, provided a steady business for Christy's Funeral Home, which has been in operation by the Christy family since 1898. Today Christy's continues to bury the dead of the *Third Ward* and the rest of the city. Matt Christy, the current proprietor, said the first funeral home was located on Church and Broad streets. Shortly after the turn of the century, the business was moved to 1 E. Broad Street, where it remained in operation until it moved to its current location, 11 E. Broad Street, in 1986. Christy, now 79, lived for 13 years in the *Third Ward* before he went off to military school.

The Christy boys. All three Christy cousins became funeral directors. (Photo taken about 1917). From left to right: Daniel Christy (Elmer, N.J.) (Now, Adams Funeral Home); Horace Christy (Woodstown, NJ) (no longer in operation); Paul B. Christy Sr., (Millville, NJ). Millville Christy Funeral Home is the only one still operating with the original name.

He remembers the Third Ward as a simpler, safer time. "People didn't lock their houses," Christy said. "They could get a skeleton key for a dime." That key would open any door to any house. Factory workers walked to their jobs. Each neighborhood seemed to have its own school, bar and church. In the *Third Ward*, there was *St. Mary's Catholic Church*, and the *Second Methodist Church*. Not only were they separate denominations, they were separate neighborhoods. Somehow, they learned to interact happily. People planted vegetables in their yards, and it was not unusual to see farm animals on a neighbor's land. Christy recalls owning several hound dogs for hunting. Neighbors would walk seamlessly through each others' yards. There were no real barriers. Families were close because they had to be. The bars – such as those located at the Eagles and the Elks, were a mainstay for the men.

"They had pretty monotonous (factory) jobs," Christy said. "They worked six days a week. Children's deaths were not a rarity back then, he said.

A hearse at Christy's Funeral Home on Broad Street.

"The kids were lucky if they made it to the eighth grade." Christy should know – his family buried these children, and their death certificates reflected their young ages.

Christy's family conducted funerals when viewings were held in the home, dating as recently as the 1960s. Since many of the company houses had small doors, caskets sometimes had to be pushed through a window. "We would carry all the living room furniture upstairs. We would put up drapes and for the Catholic families, we would have kneelers, a crucifix and two candle stands." In the summertime, funerals in the home could be tricky. Christy said they would have vats of ice, with large fans blowing the cool air into the room. When there was a death in a family, the neighbors would immediately rally around the bereaved, with food and consolation.

Christy's Funeral Home has been a mainstay not only of the Third Ward, but the entire city. But because it is actually located in the *Third Ward*, residents there claim it as their own. Over the years it has serviced every possible kind of funeral. In 1969, the girlfriend of a Pagan's motorcycle club member died, Christy recalled. Since a large gathering of Pagan bikers was expected, the police were put on notice. As it turned out, a massive gathering of Pagan bikers came to pay their respects. The mourners, dressed in denim and leather, roared into Millville, and gathered at the cemetery. "They were all very well behaved," Christy recalled. The *cemetery* to which Christy referred was Mount Pleasant Cemetery on W. Main Street, the site of many *Third Ward* burials.

CHRISTY FUNERAL HOME

(Since 1898)
Matthias H. Christy, Manager, N.J.Lic. No. 2533
11 W. Broad Street • P O Box 128
Millville, New Jersey 08332
(856) 825 - 0314

Then....
l. to r. Paul B. Christy Sr., age 4; Christy Funeral Home Founder Matthias H. Christy, and wife L. Rebecca, circa 1912.

*Today....*Christy Funeral Home

*This ad for Christy's Funeral Home shows how the establishment [
Looked at the turn of the century.*

Photo courtesy of the Christy family.

Smallpox Scare

The flu epidemic wasn't the first health scare in the city. Millville history buff Terry Pangburn offered a newspaper photo dated March 27, 1915, headlined:

"SIDELIGHT ON THE SMALLPOX SCARE."

It showed men on top of the roof of a house. The caption under the photo stated: "This house and family in Millville, N. J., have been put under quarantine, so the masculine members there of being barred from their usual activities are seeking what the recreation and amusement may be obtained from the roof top. The hours are whiled away by exchanging gossip and badinage with sympathetic passersby." Although the caption does not give the address of the house, Pangburn noted, "If I were to venture a guess, I would say that it looks very similar to the *company houses* that were built in the *Third Ward.*"

The Philadelphia Evening Ledger reported:
"New Jersey Town's Board of Health Criticized for Its Methods in Dealing with Quarantine and Vaccination Problems."

"Two thousand men and boys were thrown out of work today, by the closing of the Whitall Tatum Glass Works, when it was found that one of the employees had smallpox. He is Ellwood Charlesworth, of Plum Street, south Millville." Apparently, the city was taken to task for not adhering to a strict quarantine policy. A general vaccination of all Millville residents was urged, at the expense of the city. "So far the board has absolutely refused to do this, and the 11 physicians in the town are reaping a harvest," the paper reported.

"Any Inhabitant of Millville who wishes to be inoculated against smallpox must pay for it himself. The prices range from 50 cents to $1, and in some instances, it is said, there have been charges of $2. The physicians are working from early in the morning until late at night vaccinating citizens, and are averaging $50 to $100 a day in fees. It was charged that the Board of Health hesitated to call for general vaccination at the expense of the city because it wished to protect the physicians, who refused to talk about the matter. They are too busy vaccinating."

The pox hit the city's industries hard.

"The Whitall Tatum plant will be fumigated today and employees will be permitted to return to work when they are vaccinated," the paper reported.

Orders of products exported from Millville fell dramatically, due to the fear of infection. Millville merchants are losing thousands of dollars daily it is estimated, as a result to the epidemic.

The Blizzard of 1888

Millville did not escape *The Great Blizzard of 1888*, which raged from March 11 to March 14 and dumped some 20-60 inches of snow in the Northeast. Winds of more than 45 mph produced snowdrifts more than 50 feet. It paralyzed the region, shutting down railroads and people trapped in their homes for nearly a week, many without electricity. The storm must have paralyzed news coverage too, since there is not much written about the blizzard. At least one local man froze to death. There was no mail delivery.

On March, 15, 1888, *The Bridgeton Evening News* reported succinctly on the great blizzard of 1888:

"Wanted: Communication with the outside world."

The storm spared no creature from its wrath. On March 12th, *The Bridgeton Evening News* reported in poignant detail how the blizzard affected even the tiniest of creatures.

"Several sparrows were picked off the streets this morning encased in snow and ice – dead. They resembled little balls of ice and snow, but when opened, the poor little birds were found within."

Early newspapers often mixed tragic news alongside the lighter side of life. On the same page, The News reported:

"A *Third Ward* chap, who wanted to see his sweetheart some nights since, accidentally interviewed her papa. The meeting must have been short, sharp and decisive as the chap is said to have jumped the front yard fence in his haste to get away from that neighborhood."

The Candy Man

Let's talk candy. It seems like there was no shortage of candy shops in the *Third Ward*. At least there were as many candy shops as bars. Former youngsters still fondly remember their favorites. Although not all of them were located in the *Third Ward* proper, some mom-and-pop stores hugged the fringes of the Ward. Many Third Warders vividly recall the special daily pilgrimage to their favorite candy store after school to satisfy their sweet tooth. And they remember the names of the penny candies that are no more.

"I used to go to Frank's on Archer Street when I went to Wood School," said former Third Warder Terry Pangburn. "It was then owned by Frank Kesterson and his wife. Later on, Flossie O'Neill opened a store in that same location. Favorite candy? BB Bat Taffies and Bonimo Turkish Taffies."

Lillian Kimberlin, principal of Wood School

Maryjane Lloyd Moats said, "I loved *Huntley's* on Church Street. He had the best penny candy and would let you come behind the counter to pick out what you wanted. Annie Burke's was on Sharp Street between Church and North."

Two favorite spots for children were *Goldie's* and *Huntley's*. Bruce Higgins said he loved *Huntley's* "candy cigarettes and mini-wax coke bottles with the juice inside." If perchance you weren't interested in candy, a rarity, you could snag a comic book.

The candy stores were a cornucopia of sweet riches for Paula Price, who said she remembers them all: *Millie's*; *Betty's*; *Giuffra*; and *Goldie's*. "I loved them all," she said. "I frequented *Betty's* more because I lived closer. I would go to *Betty's* with $1 and get a three-pack of chocolate Tastykakes and Pepsi – and get change! I'd bring my soda bottle back to get my nickel deposit and buy five penny candies."

For Suzy Schwegel, there were two favorite shops: She visited Burke's on Sharp Street every day, spending her allowance or pennies from her mother's change. *Annie*, was her second favorite. "Annie would invite me to come behind the counter and bag my own," Schwegel said. "For Easter and Christmas Mom and Dad went to Frank Giuffra's on High Street. Loved their coconut cream dark chocolate eggs and an item Frank Guiffra called 'pheasant eggs.' They were about the size of a jelly bean but with a coconut cream inside the candy shell. I never found them any place again after the fire that destroyed Guiffra's candy store in the 1980s. My mom and dad were the best Easter bunnies! I can still taste that candy! Oh ...and there was always a chocolate cross in each basket!"

Everyone seems to have memories of their favorite penny candies – which, if they are still made today – are surely no longer a penny.

Andy Stover shared this photo of the Wood School Safety patrol, late 1930s. Andy Stover's father, George Stover is in the first row, far right.

Photo courtesy of Andy Stover

Michele Kirksey's favorite was *Swedish fish*. For Gay Taylor it was *Mary Janes*. For Doris Tomlin, her favorites were the little

Gold Rush bags of gum and the bars of taffy – vanilla, chocolate, strawberry or banana."

Of course today's speedy convenience stores – Wawa, Seven-Eleven, etc. have replaced the mom-and-pop candy stores. The idea of a *penny candy* is a mere memory, and hired clerks have replaced both *mom* and *pop*.

Former Third Warder Charles "Chick" Bennett recalls his favorite store – *Huntley's*. "It sat between 615 and 609 Church St.," Bennett said. "It was directly across the street from the old Fire House. I lived in 400 W Powell St. at the corner of Church and Powell about a half -block from *Huntley's.*

"When you walked to the store, the door was in the middle of the front of the building. You walked on a floor that creaked as you walked. There was an aisle to your left that led to the cash register. Just a couple of steps before the cash register and to the right of the aisle was a bubble gum machine that contained small colored balls of bubble gum. There was a special colored ball; it was yellow with a red stripe around it. This was the one that was the goal of all of us kids to get. If you got this ball you would give it to Mr. Huntley and were able to pick out any 5-cent candy bar. My cousin Sam Bennett and our pal Buddy Abdel, (his real name was Carl A. Abdel) and I would always pick a Three Musketeers Bar. It was made in a way that it could be broken into three equal pieces – a piece for all three of us."

Across the street from St. Mary's School, there was *Shannon's Candy Store*, which later became the very popular *Shannon's Sub Shop*, another Millville institution. The neighborhood kids used to go to the candy store and get a good-sized bag of candy for about a nickel. You could even get a pack of baseball cards with a stick of bubble gum inside for five cents.

Jackie Menz Abbott lived at 105 W. McNeal St. in the 1940s and 1950s, she said. "We used to go to Mr. Bailey's store on the same side of the street as us down near Archer Street. My father would send us to the store to buy cigarettes for him which were 17 cents a pack. My brother Paul Menz and I would also buy candy – my favorite was *Root Beer Barrels* and *Tootsie Pops* and *candy cigarettes*. Sometimes we would buy cigarettes for ourselves and go smoke them in the woods at the end of Dock Street, before Arlene Village (apartment complex) was there."

Dedication of the Arlene Village apartments in the 1950s.
The developer named it after his daughter.
The city has since razed it.

Pat Caruso, who lived on McNeal Street, said, "I remember a corner store on High and Foundry Streets called *TROPPS*. The owners lived in the back of the store. They had one part where you could go in the second part of the store and pick a gift for your birthday or good report cards. They even gave you choices of candy or ice cream for every good grade you got on your report cards. They were very nice people. Then at Easter and Christmas especially we would go to *Giuffra's*. They did have the best dark chocolate covered coconut cream eggs. One year the fellow I was dating at the time went there and had a five-pound dark chocolate coconut cream egg for Easter. Man I loved those two places the best!"

The Hess Murder

Although police records from the 1950s are sketchy, residents who lived in the *Bloody Third* recall other incidents of violence. Many people mistakenly point to the 1950 murder of teenager Lorraine Hess as the incident that sparked the name *Bloody Third*. The Porreco case actually preceded the Hess murder by decades. Also, the Hess murder did not occur in the *Third Ward*. Because many Millville residents incorrectly believe the infamous crime occurred in the *Third Ward*, we are including it here. The crime dominated both local and national newspapers and magazines.

According to the May 14, 1950 issue of the *Chicago Tribune*, Lorraine, 17, was on her way home from a school play when she was murdered. Her body was found by a neighbor on May 13th. The pretty brunette had not been raped, but was strangled, apparently by her own belt. The Millville High School junior was found between two houses on Sassafras Street, which is not located in the *Third Ward*. A young man named Ted Carter, a factory worker, was convicted of the crime, although many people believed him innocent. The true-crime magazine *Front Page Detective* reported that although Carter was 18, he had a mental capacity of a 9-year-old. Indeed, many believe he was framed. The magazine wrote that Carter was convicted on flimsy evidence and even hinted that he may have been framed. It quoted one Millville resident who supposedly knew more about the crime than he let on. "What do you want me to do?" it quoted the person. "Don't forget that I still live in Millville." The magazine declared: "Meanwhile, according to many of the long-term residents of South Jersey, the real killer is still placidly roaming the pleasant streets of Millville."

The crime was considered infamous at a time when the slaying of an innocent female student was a rarity. Although sentenced to life in prison for the 1950 murder of Lorraine Hess, N.J. Department of Correction records show he was paroled in

1967. Since his birth date is listed as June 6, 1932, he was only 36 when he re-entered the public. The DOC records list the case as simply "closed" in 1977.

For the many people who believe Ted Carter was innocent of the Hess murder, they will be happy to know he found some measure of happiness after leaving prison. According to Millville resident D. Renne Brecht, Ted Carter was her aunt's second husband.

"Ted passed away several years ago. He was living on Hogbin Road at the time," Brecht wrote on Facebook's "Millville Memory Lane."

Accidental Violence

There was also the occasional case of accidental violence. In the late 1800s and the early part of the 20th century, there was no shortage of guns in the *Third Ward* – and not all were used for hunting.

In one *Third Ward* incident, a gentleman by the name of Benjamin Wilson was shot in a freak accident by James McCorriston on July 19, 1892. Newspaper accounts at the time recounted the incident, reporting that McCorriston was standing on Buck Street, in front of his father's store when he shot his rifle at a bird that was on Wilson's back fence. Wilson's residence was on the east side of Dock Street, north of Powell Street. Wilson had just returned home from work and was taking a leisurely, relaxing jaunt through his back yard garden, bending over and admiring his flowers. Newspaper accounts say that Wilson "raised up just in time to get the contents of the rifle which McCorriston fired, and fell as though dead."

The account goes on: "McCorriston, when he found what he had done, was nearly wild with grief, and McCorriston's father has done all in power to help the suffering man, Wilson."

The article stated that "Doctors Jones, Wheaton, and Newell have done all in their power to locate the ball, but have only followed it to the entrance of the brain. The ball entered just back of the left ear and took a sloping course." They called in an expert physician. Finally, the article stated that "At this writing, Wilson is no better, but the physician is expected within half hour and may be able to locate the ball." Whether poor Wilson died or not is not known. The newspaper article went on to report that a three-masted schooner was loading clay, and then announced an upcoming wedding.

There were a number of freak accidents in the *Third Ward*. A boat accident on June 28, 1916 left a *Third Ward* man seriously injured. According to The Bridgeton Evening News, George Stover

Jr. of Sharp Street was badly burned when a gasoline engine in a boat exploded, igniting his clothes and setting the boat on fire.

The boat reportedly was floating near the Sharp Street Bridge and Stover was cranking up the engine when it backfired and exploded, burning his hands. He was able to make it to shore, but not without severe burns. The boat burned near the water's edge.

Domestic incidents and neighborhood brawls in the *Third Ward* were not uncommon. One February Saturday night in 1888, a fight broke out at Broad Street and Columbia Avenue. According to newspaper accounts:

"John Moss rushed from the other side of the street with an open pen knife and stabbed William Adams twice in the abdomen and once in the side. There were no officers present, and Adams was carried home."

Police arrested Moss the next day. Adams wasn't seriously injured and remarked "that he was pretty full the night before."

The newspaper stated:

"Of course, rum and beer was the cause of all the trouble."

The Great Cotton Mill Fire

Millville Fire Chief Kurt Hess, who grew up across town from the *Third Ward*, remembers the *Third Ward* as a forbidden place. Hess's family is steeped in the history of the Millville Fire Department; his father and grandfather were high-ranking firefighters. Growing up, Hess recalls that "the *Third Ward* had such a bad reputation, we weren't allowed to be there. Those kids, in the *Third Ward*, went to Wood School. There were always gang fights. I wasn't allowed past Second Street."

Hess recalls the landscape of the Third Ward: "Everything was built around the cotton mill."

Indeed, the mill created Union Lake, one of the largest manmade lakes in the state, and built the dam to generate energy to the mill. The workers lived in company housing, neat duplexes adjacent to the mill, and the mill officials lived in ornate houses on Columbia Avenue.

"I think the urban culture of the Third Ward started there," Hess said.

Even though they may not have lived there, generations of Hess men fought fires in the *Third Ward*. Millville didn't have an officially organized fire company until 1888. The current firehouse was dedicated on Jan. 19, 1957. Over the years, the fire company gained a reputation as one of the best in the state of New Jersey.

Millville Fire Department #2

Like many other firefighters, Hess remembers the burning of the huge nearly-abandoned structure as the most sensational fire to ever strike the city. Hess recalled that the day of the big cotton mill fire – Nov. 3, 1976; City firefighters were attending their monthly meeting in the fire hall when the alarm went off around 7:15 p.m. Hess, a young firefighter at the time, rode at the back of the fire truck. "By the time we turned on Broad Street you could see the fire," he said. The behemoth mill, string of buildings, was a setting for the perfect fire, with its oil-soaked floors and the draft from a huge paddle wheel used to procure hydro-electricity power. Add to that the giant pottery kilns inside the building, and it was clear the blaze had the upper hand against the firefighters. The mammoth flames, playing leapfrog with each other, made the night-

time scene appear like the "burning of Atlanta" scene in "Gone with the Wind." No firefighters were very seriously injured, but they worked in exhaustion past dawn to get the fire under control. The entire city seemed to come out to watch the spectacle. The old cotton mill was just beginning to take on a new life as a pottery barn.

The old mill dated back to 1854, when safety regulations were not as strict as they are today. All four floors of the building were engulfed by flames by the time firefighters arrived at the scene. The building was composed of stone walls and timbers, a foot-by-6-inches in size. According to mill officials, during its heyday – the Civil War – there were about 25,000 spindles and 500 looms in the mill. Also in its height, the mill employed about 600 people.

At the time of the blaze, the mill was nearly abandoned. The Wood family closed it, and phased out the Millville Manufacturing Company – where so many Third Warders had been employed. The main building — there were several – was purchased by the

Wheaton Industries. Frank Wheaton Jr., owner of Dorchester Pottery Inc., told reporters that about 40 people were employed on the first floor. The pottery workers were able to flee the fire. The rest of the building was empty.

There were fire companies from every section of the county fighting the flames. One firefighter was slightly hurt, but there were no major injuries. Wheaton couldn't put a dollar amount on the damage, although he said it was substantial. He had made a major capital investment, including specially-made equipment shipped over from Europe. Wheaton called it "Dorchester Pottery Inc."

An equally-devastating effect of the fire was the threat it  posed to the *Third Ward*. "I don't think many people then or now realize just how near of a true disaster the fire could have been, and how close it was to losing the entire *Third Ward*," Everett John Hoffman, a lifelong fire and rescue officer recalled. Hoffman was one of the hundreds of firefighters that battled the blaze.

According to some news reports, embers from the massive blaze fell like snow on the century-old factory homes built by the Wood family for workers at the mill. Many homeowners near the fire brought out their garden hoses to wet down their homes. Adding to the trouble was a gusty wind that blew embers into the Third Ward.

The massive blaze also threatened several of the historic mansion houses on Columbia Avenue. The office building at 821 Columbia Avenue was shared by the Maurice River Company and James R. Hurley Associates.

I was a young reporter for *The Bridgeton Evening News* assigned to cover the fire. I got a bit too close to it, and I found myself covered in heat blisters the next day. Nelson was there too, among the many spectators who watched in awe and disbelief as the fire burned through the night.

"It seemed to burn forever," Hess recalled. The company mill – around which the entire Third Ward had once revolved – had been reduced to a pile of debris and ashes.

Like hundreds of other area residents, Linda Morgan recalls watching the mammoth blaze from her home on Church Street – right on corner of Broad and Church streets, where her family had a Sonic Flite Archery business. Her memories echo all those who gathered to watch the once-thriving industrial mill burn into ruins.

"When the fire first happened I just lived down the street. My kitchen door was lit up, like a bright orange glass," Morgan recalled. "I wondered: What the heck? The sky was orange. You could see the flames and the smoke and then the fire trucks. I had never seen a fire that big before! My then-husband Bobby and I started running down to be sure there wasn't anyone in the mill. My grandmother had worked there. The fire was so big and so scorching, it singed my hair and burned my face like sunburn.

"It went on for hours. It was an amazing sight. As far as I remember no one died. It may have been empty at the time. The day after, it was still smoking "

At the time of the cotton mill fire, Hoffman was a young Millville firefighter, who just happened to be at the fire hall that night. "I had enlisted in the U.S. Coast Guard several months earlier and had been temporarily stationed at Fortescue and Cape May Search and Rescue (SAR) stations and was home on leave," he said.

Hoffman recalls in chilling detail how firefighters first heard of the blaze.

"Nearly the entire department of the MFD was assembled at the firehouse for their monthly meeting including my dad, Everett Hoffman, Jr., who by that time had nearly 20 years of service under his belt," Hoffman said. "Membership in the fire department at that time was restricted to those 21 and older and many younger guys like myself, joined the squad at age 16 or 17. I had enlisted in the U.S. Coast Guard several months earlier and had been temporarily stationed at Fortescue and Cape May SAR stations and was home on leave.

"Several of us were hanging around at the squad building in the early evening including myself, Wes Morgan, Joe McMahon, Sr. and a few others. We heard the alarm sound for a fire and almost instantly several trucks were rounding the corner of Buck and Vine

Streets and heading up Columbia Avenue. Even before any radio traffic could be heard on the magnitude of the fire, flames and the bright orange glow in the sky could be seen from the squad building in the direction the fire apparatus were traveling.

"Someone quickly sounded the squad's alarm from the watch room (this was before county dispatch and 911) while the rest of us scrambled to staff the squad's ambulances and rescue truck and headed up Columbia Avenue. Several fire apparatus had entered into the Mill complex and were operating from the river side, other additional apparatus were arriving out on Columbia Avenue as the size and intensity of the fire was like nothing we'd ever seen. Fire Chief George Schoch was striking multiple alarms as he was requesting additional resources from other departments. Large embers were being carried by the wind across Columbia Avenue and into the entire *Third Ward*. The larger wood frame houses directly across the street from the Mill on Columbia were being threatened with radiant heat and embers. I remember Firefighter Jack Reeves, one of the career guys, operating MFDs 1952 LaFrance Invader, Engine 36, on Columbia Avenue, and he directed Wes Morgan and I to grab a hose line and start wetting down the structures on the north side of Columbia.

"The size of the fire seemed to continue to grow and the amount of manpower, water, and apparatus needed to overcome the fire seemed nearly impossible to bring things under control. At some point, the N.J. Forest Fire Service arrived and began doing ember patrols in the Third Ward as Wes and I were relieved of our cooling down job. With the main fire progressing to an outbuilding closer to Columbia directly in front of Engine 36 operated by Reeves, a 2.5 inch hose line laid at the ready on the sidewalk. By this time, some mutual aid fire departments had begun to arrive in the city and a fire officer from the City of Vineland approached Wes and I to go into service with the 2.5 inch line on the building directly in front of us. Neither Wes or I had yet been to fire school and really didn't know what to expect when operating a large caliber hose stream.. We were 18 and 19 years old, strong and fit but not necessarily brutes to handle the force of a large bore straight stream without some experience.

"We picked up the line, and not knowing anything about nozzle reaction, we yanked back on the bail of the nozzle which quickly overwhelmed us and took both of us to the ground. We wrestled with the line for a few seconds until we could regain control and our footing. At one point, I remember looking back at Reeves as he got a good laugh at our struggle. We moved forward with the line and stayed in service with it until we had knocked down what could from that point.

This fire was extremely dangerous and had all the potential to injure and kill those working it along with burning down much of the *Third Ward.* I had not seen my dad and wasn't sure where he was assigned. Later that night I had an opportunity to get around to the back side of the main Mill structure (on the river side) and located my dad operating the 1973 Grove Ladder truck. The ladder was up and its ladder pipe was in service playing a large stream of water on the main building where they operated for hours. I had an opportunity to chat with him for a few minutes relaying what had been the scene on Columbia Avenue while he described his side of the fire.

"It was a long night, and we never did get to go to bed; somewhere around 5 in the morning I left to go home, showered, donned my Coast Guard uniform and reported back to Cape May for duty. The mill fire had been a spectacular scene; and the efforts of the Millville Fire Department along with the assistance of many others, gave evidence of a tremendous fight to keep the fire contained."

Even though that May another fire would break out in another mill building, it couldn't compare with the ferocious fire of that November night. Up until that time, the Bellamy Hotel fire, at the corner of High and Main, where the Jaycee Senior High Rise now is, was considered the largest fire in the city. There had been other memorable fires – such as the icy winter blaze that destroyed the historic Giuffra Candy Store on High Street on a bitterly icy cold February day in 1985. But no fire could compare to the original cotton mill fire, according to Hess.

Many others agree with Hoffman: No one in the *Third Ward* realized how close they came to losing their homes had it not been for the tireless efforts of the firefighters, who stayed at the scene past the point of exhaustion.

Today Hoffman is fire chief of the Washington Township Fire Department and industrial safety instructor, continuing education at Gloucester County College. He still considers the cotton mill fire as one of the major incidents in his career.

"This is how the remnants of the old cotton mill on Columbia Avenue look today, boarded up and abandoned."

The Bars

It seems more workers may have frequented the bars than the churches. According to Wright-Hinson:

"There were a lot of problems with drinking, and there were always lots of fights going on. People would get under each other's skin at work, and it carried over to home; put alcohol on top of that, and you had a volatile environment."

Coach Andrews as a Boy Scout

Well-known Millville High School "Coach" Ed Andrews was born and raised in four different homes in the Third Ward. He remembers each as a "rough, tough neighborhood," which consisted of factory workers, either at the glass factories, the cotton mill or Armstrong Cork. His parents, Irene and Allen Jr., never drove an automobile. "We walked everywhere."His father worked at the cotton mill. When his shift was over, he headed to one of the many local bars, such as John's Bar, or the Third Ward Tavern, for hours. "My mother would tell me to go down to the bar to get my father. Any 'free time' my father had, was always spent at the bar," he said. That was not an uncommon ritual. Indeed, that was the pattern for many families whose fathers worked shift work. There was no shortage of alcohol-fueled domestic brawls.

Ken Butcher, of Galveston, Texas, whose family bought the infamous *Third Ward Tavern* in 1977, was able to turn a raucous establishment into a more respectable place, although the shift workers from the glass houses still frequented the bar. Built before the turn of the century, it was located at Foundry and Church streets.

This was once the home of the wildly popular Third Ward Tavern.

Butcher's family was able to qualm many of the bloody brawls and turn the Third Ward Tavern into a respectable neighborhood bar. But it wasn't totally without its share of commotion, Butcher said.

"Shift workers would come in about 8 or 9 a.m. We had a lot of Wheaton (Glass) workers," Butcher recalled. "They would come in sober and drink themselves sober. It was 50 cents a glass. One guy would come in there and sit there and drink all day. About 3 p.m. he would be drunk and at 5 p.m. he would be sober as anything."

Carol Keller, beloved proprietor of the Third Ward Tavern, is shown here behind the bar after her family took over the establishment in 1977.. Her son said she reigned over the bar like a queen over her kingdom. Just as in older days, the bar opened early in the morning to accommodate the glass workers who were just finishing their shifts.

Photo courtesy of Butch Keller

Ken's mother Carol was the beloved matriarch of the bar. "She was loved by everyone," Ken said. She presided over the tavern like a queen over her kingdom. "If someone didn't have enough money to pay, she'd serve them anyway."

Unlike the old always-rowdy days of the tavern, bar fights were kept in check by the owners. "The bar was still rough when we took over," Ken admitted, "but we didn't condone fights. Any problems, I'd just show them the door. Out they went. We didn't call the police. We took care of our own problems."

And this book wouldn't be complete without a nod to Otto's Bar on E. Main Street. It may not have been located in the *Third Ward*, but it was haven to many *Third Ward* workers ending a grueling shift. It was particularly popular because it was a *men's only* bar. Women were, politely, simply not served. One former *Third Ward* female resident said, "We loved Otto's because we knew our husbands were safe. From other women —you know. If they were at Otto's, the only trouble they could get into was drinking too much."

Micki Gilbert Merritt said, "My Dad used to go there for a beer with the guys! He took my daughter when she was only a toddler in 1971 to show her off! Only girl in the place!"

Eric Conova said, "My dad, Santo and his friend, Bill Morey, had seats with their names on them. One of my early memories was police officers sitting at the bar in uniform having a few. I'm assuming they were off duty. I was an officer in later years, and that would have gotten me fired."

Bonnie Reynolds was one of the rare, brave women who walked through the doors of Otto's Bar – but not for a drink.

"When I was the Director of Cumberland County Homeless, I was called on a Friday afternoon and advised a couple that was homeless in the area of Otto's Bar could be placed in housing if I could get them to the Housing Authority that afternoon. If they did not go in before they closed that day, the unit would be given to someone else, Reynolds recalled.

"I searched all the areas they were known to frequent but to no avail. The only other spot was Otto's Bar that I really did not want to even consider. Knowing the reputation of 'No Women,' but also realizing the urgency of finding the couple, I swallowed hard and walked into the bar, looking neither left or right but straight ahead. Unfortunately, they were not there so I made a hasty retreat and headed back to my office in Bridgeton. As I entered my office the phone was ringing and the person on the other end asked me if I had just been in Otto's Bar. News certainly did travel fast!"

Reynolds noted, "The story had a happy ending," and she was able to place the couple in a unit after all.

"Al's Bar," at Buck and Broad streets, was a true *Third Ward* bar. It could be rowdy at times. Now a community center, the bar was a favorite watering hole for shift workers. Sonny Craner said, "Otto's was 'Old School,' like Al's Bar. Still remember the *Ladies Entrance* on the side of Al's. My mom would take us kids to pick up my dad, and we were expected to stay in the *back room.* "

Craner remembered that "The *gentlemen* sat at the bar and the *ladies* had their own entrance on the side that led directly to the back room. They would serve the women through an opening at the back of the bar. Al Driscoll and his wife Laura ran the place, and were very, very nice folks. Occasionally, when there weren't many patrons, Al would allow us to come into the *Bar room* and we thought that was the coolest thing ever!"

Artistic Endeavors

Third Ward was also home for a time for famed artist Pat Witt.

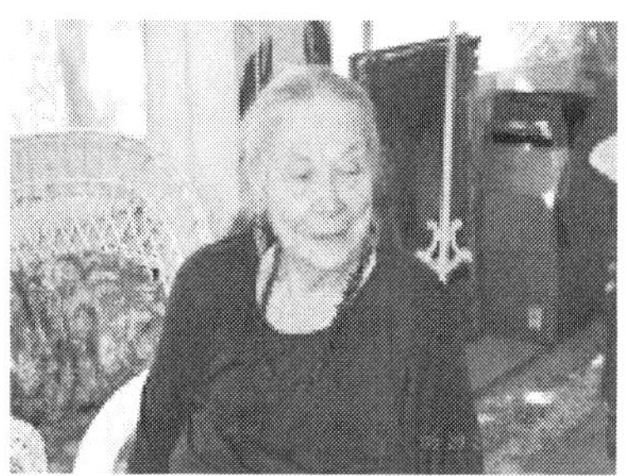

*Pat Witt, known as Millville's Artist Laureate,
lived for a brief time in the Third Ward while growing up.
She has fond memories of her time on Sharp Street.*

Photo courtesy of Chick Bennett

Known as Millville's' Artist Laureate, she is also known as Wetlands Painter, particularly for her stunningly beautiful paintings of the river and marshlands in Cumberland County. She opened the renowned *Barn Studio of Art* in Millville in 1962. Thousands of budding artists – and their children and grandchildren –became professionals under her tutorage. Witt, now 88, lived in a half double at 216 Sharp Street in the *Third Ward*, from 1958 to 1962. In 1962 she moved to her current address and opened the hugely successful art studio.

During an interview on her porch at the secluded Barn Studio of Art – surrounded by flowers and birds and cats – Witt recalled her time on Sharp Street with a smile. Serendipitously, her mother, a school teacher, lived two doors down from her on Sharp Street. It was a time when children could play outside after dark, and no one locked their doors. Witt recalled the *Third Ward* as "a happy place. There was absolutely nothing scary about it," she said. Even after she moved from the *Third Ward*, she maintained close ties to the area. An avid volunteer, Witt gave hundreds of hours of her time to various groups too numerous to mention here. Her house – which

Witt used as a canvas to express her individuality – was always abuzz with creative people, and Witt was happy to entertain them. Her then-neighbor, Suzy Schwegel, recalled Witt with great fondness.

"She had the neatest house. I loved the way she had it decorated. I spent many hours with her. She taught me how to make a rag rug and later became my agent as a baby sitter. She found me my first jobs among her friends who were young mothers," Schwegel said. "She's a great lady who years later also helped my nephew John with his art career. She most definitely was a part of our Third Ward for a while."

Today Witt is world-known, and has been the subject of several documentaries. Her *Barn* is tucked neatly in a quiet enclave in Millville. Generations of artists have passed through her doors and still flock there today. "There's a kind of 'bubble' over this place," Witt said. "I need this positive energy. It's very spiritual here."

On November, 3, 1976 a friend of Witt's called her to tell her about the raging fire at the old cotton mill. "I went right down there," Witt recalled. "I knew I had to sketch something right away. I asked the fire chief if I could get closer and I did." Fearlessly and frantically, armed only with a pad and pencils, she sketched the fire as it lit up the Millville sky. "I knew I had to capture it right away," Witt said. "I knew the next morning the cotton mill would be gone. And I was right." The resulting painting is a haunting reminder of the mammoth blaze that roared in the Third Ward. Firefighters were fearful – and rightfully so – about flying embers endangering the Third Ward houses. In the painting, Witt captured the devastation of the mill as no photo can.

The painting of the cotton mill factory fire by artist Pat Witt

She was granted a front-row seat by the fire chief so she could capture the night on canvas.

*Renowned artist Pat Witt displays her painting
of the great cotton mill factory fire in November 1976.
She was offered many lucrative offers for the painting,
but refuses to sell.*

Photo courtesy of Chick Bennett

Although the cotton mill had long been closed, there still were pottery workers at the compound at the time of the fire. Fortunately, no one was seriously injured in the blaze. But the fire – and subsequent demolishing of the mill's remnants – marked the official end of an era for the Third Ward.

Memories

Not all of the *"Bloody Third's"* history involved liquor or crime. There are some personal anecdotes from residents and relatives of residents who offer amazing personal tales about the old *Third Ward*.

Before Wawa, there were mom and pop candy stores, seemingly on every corner in the *Third Ward*: *Huntley's* on Church Street; *Burke's* on Sharp Street; *the Bond Store* on North Street. Hershey milk chocolate bars were a nickel, but the penny candy was the best. What a great assortment! Spread out in front of young eager kids like a confectionary cornucopia at Thanksgiving. Those days, of course, are but a memory.

Michelle Wright-Hinson alluded to the *Third Ward* workers employed by R.D. Wood, who owned the cotton mills on Columbia Avenue.

*Forget 'Rosie the Riveter'! These ladies worked
at the cotton mills long before WWII.*

Photo courtesy of Dale Wettstein

"The company paid their employees with copper coins that were only good in the company store and the bar. It (the *Third Ward*) was its own community. The company owned a store; the bar; and they had their own fire department, and the church, which is still there." The old fire department still stands on Church Street.

The Millville Fire Department Resolution Hose No. 3 at Diligence Hall on Church Street has its trucks decorated for a patriotic holiday.

Photo courtesy of Dale Wettstein

Lest anyone get the impression that Third Ward homes were all tainted by alcohol, it should be noted that many residents have fond childhood memories of the *Third Ward*. Kathy Horseman, who now lives in Port Norris, Cumberland County, not far from Millville, said both her parents worked in the Wheaton Glass plant. She lived in a duplex at 507 Sharp St., where she stayed until she married at 18.

She still harbors wonderful memories of growing up in the city's *Third Ward*. In fact, remembers her toddlerhood as a personal fairyland.

"Every Wednesday, my father would marry me," she said with a chuckle. "My sister would put a special dress on me, and I'd walk down the *aisle* to my father. And we'd get married. My father would collect change over the week, and that was for my *reception*. He'd take me to Annie Burke's candy store and I could spend my money. It was all penny candy back then. If he gave me a quarter, I'd have 25 pieces of candy."

The wedding ritual lasted from kindergarten up until she was about 10 years old. "When I learned to ride (a bicycle), my father got me a bike for our *anniversary*." Horseman recalls both her parents as doting and loving and her childhood nothing less than ideal.

There were no shootings and no violent fights, although the boys might rumble from time to time, but disagreements soon were resolved and no one held a grudge.

"Everyone was friendly. Everyone hung out at our house. I remember Christmas time, walking down High Street and doing my Christmas shopping. I was never afraid. I would have to say I had the best childhood ever," Horseman said.

Judi Grau Shute offered her own memory of winter fun.

"I would sled on Clay Hill, down by the river behind my house. Just a short walk through the woods. Mom would only let me go with my older sister and her friends - I'm sure they were thrilled! My afternoons were spent shoveling snow from sidewalks at Roosevelt Park. Fifty cents, twenty five cents was about the going rate. Now I'm happy just staying inside with a warm good memory!"

Police Shooting

Over recent years, the *Third Ward* has periodically erupted in violence involving domestic disputes. Once such incident involved the fatal shooting of a Millville man by city police.

On October 1, 1981, Millville Police fatally shot Daniel Petrick, 21, of Vine Street after he tried to shoot his wife Wendy Petrick, 18, as she sat in a pickup truck in the parking lot of the former Wawa store on Sharp Street. According to news reports, one of the shots went through the side of the truck and struck Wendy in the head. She was taken to the hospital where she was treated for a minor head injury and released.

However, the chase of Daniel Petrick by police had just begun. Daniel Patrick rode his bike to his mother's house on Vine Street, where he lived. According to news reports, he fled upstairs to a second-floor bathroom.

Millville Police officers Bill Narvaez and Paul McIsaac, along with then-Detective Ronald Harvey arrived at the house, and headed up the narrow stairway leading to the bathroom. As they approached, news reports stated, Petrick swung open the bathroom and assumed a shooting position.

Then, according to reports, Narvaez fired one shotgun blast and McIsaac fired two shots from his 38 caliber service revolver. Petrick was wounded in his lower abdomen and thigh.

He was taken to Millville Hospital, where he lingered in critical condition until he subsequently died of his injuries. The shooting by police was found to be legitimate and both officers were cleared of any wrongdoing.

Neighborly friction

Even religion was a source of friction in the *Third Ward*.

According to Ken Robinson, his 92-year-old father "told me that the *Third Ward* was where the Catholics lived, and if you were a Protestant and ventured through that area, you better be ready to fight. Hence, *The Bloody Third Ward*. Street fights among boys were common in the *Third Ward*. But the day after a brawl, you could see the same boys playing stick-ball together. It was just a way of life. And no one held grudges.

Eleanor Cain speaks and looks like someone who is a fraction of her 91 years. Fiercely independent, she lives alone now in a new *active adult community* in Millville. She has clear, dancing eyes and happily retells the stories of growing up in the *Third Ward*.

Eleanor was born in the house in 1923 and lived at 101 Archer Street until she married at 23 years old. In many ways her childhood is representative of the many children who grew up in the *Third Ward* during the first half of the 19th Century. However, unlike many other children, her father didn't work in the mills. He owned his own grocery store at McNeal and North streets – until the Depression hit, and he took a Works Progress Administration job.

Eleanor was keenly aware of the plight of the other children in her neighborhood. Many of their fathers worked in the cotton mill or glass houses. That meant getting everything – from food to clothes to pots and pans – at the company store on Columbia Avenue. The workers would buy all the necessities for their homes at the company store and at the end of the week, collect whatever *pay* was left over.

All too often, the fellows in the mills or glass works would spend the remainder of their paychecks at the neighborhood bar.

"Too often, the guys would get into fights with each other because they were drunk," Eleanor recalled.

The Bloody Third

By: Eileen Bennett & Nelson Trout

But that wasn't Eleanor's world. She and her mother, father, and older sister Beulah lived in the neatly-kept half double house on Archer Street with no electricity or plumbing.

"I remember when they put electricity in our house," Eleanor said. "Up until then, we used oil lamps."

It may have been a simple time, but it wasn't easy. A bath meant heating water in a bucket downstairs and then carrying it up – sometimes as much as 20 trips – to a huge claw-foot tub upstairs.

"I loved school," Eleanor said of her time at Wood School, which she said, "always had the best teachers."

The first graduating class from R.D. Wood School, 1915.
The school celebrated its centennial in 2015 with year-long events.
Photo courtesy of Dale Wettstein

There were two main churches in the Third Ward – Second Methodist Church and St. Mary's Roman Catholic Church. Eleanor was raised as a strict Methodist. "We went to church four times on Sunday. First, for worship, then Sunday School then Youth Group meetings, and then worship again. We were not allowed to play on Sunday."

Eleanor recalls her childhood fondly.

"I knew all the people up and down the block. People kept up their houses. We didn't have a lot of toys. We made up our own entertainment."

That might mean a *crack-the-whip* game on roller skates or, in the summer, going down to Union Lake to swim. The children of the *Third Ward* were somewhat foreign to her, Eleanor said.

"My parents never said too much to me about the *Third Ward*," she said, perhaps in order to protect her from the grittiness of some of the residents. "All I know is that I had a happy childhood. I think I grew up in a good time."

*Giuffra's Snack Stand at Union Lake Park
was a favorite place for children.
Frank Giuffra later opened a poplar candy
store on High Street.*
Photo courtesy of Dale Wettstein

Never A Dull Moment

Third Warders awoke one January day during *World War II* to a most unpleasant experience – the whoosh of bullets by aircraft based at the Millville Airport, which was dedicated by the government in 1941. It opened in 1943 as a gunnery school for fighter pilots. The airport still exists today, but is no longer used as a military base.

According to newspaper accounts, the strafing of the *Third Ward* by the planes caused quite the excitement that chilly winter morning. Eight homes and a clubhouse were peppered with gunfire from military aircraft. The machine gun bullets traveled between three and four miles from the air base to the *Third Ward*.

A crash fire crew at Millville Airport, date unknown. The airport was a large part of the city's history. Eight homes and a clubhouse were accidentally peppered with gunfire from military aircraft one day in the 1940s.

The Bloody Third
By: Eileen Bennett & Nelson Trout

It was about 8:40 a.m. when the 30 rounds of ammunition were fired into the Third Ward, just as people were starting their morning chores and children were walking to school. No one was injured, but it was close, according to news accounts.

"Mary Bird, 11, and her brother, William, eight, said a bullet whizzed toward them as they walked to school," newspaper accounts reported. It was a very close call. "Mrs. Elizabeth Bean was in an upstairs area when bullets smashed a picture in the living room and knocked the legs off two chairs."

Union Lake, which hugs Third Ward, was the site of many accidental bombings. Stories abound of ammunition, weapons and even parts of planes that were found decades later in the water. At least one P-47 pilot from the Millville Airport died when his aircraft crashed into Union Lake.

A crash fire crew at Millville Airport, date unknown. The airport was a large part of the city's history. Eight homes and a clubhouse were accidentally peppered with gunfire from military aircraft one day in the 1940s.

Photo courtesy of Dale Wettstein

Also, during WWII there was an Army machine gun nest mounted on the very top of Union Lake's first cove. The gun was aimed with a perfect view of the Union Lake dam, in case of a German attack. If the dam were to burst, the Third Ward would have been severely and quickly flooded killing hundreds. The concrete pad on which the machine gun was mounted still remains, partially hidden with underbrush. It was a brutal reminder of the war.

Voting in the Bloody Third

For two and a half decades, Gladis Rhubart Mcgraw has worked at R.D. Wood School, starting as a teacher's aide and rising to the level of administrative assistant to the principal. She has become involved with a myriad of extracurricular activities through the years – always going beyond her job requirement, doing anything she can to help better the lives of the children of the *Third Ward*. Gladis herself grew up in the *Third Ward*, never forgetting her roots. She has been a tireless *champion for the kids*, a legend in her own time in many people's eyes and hearts. Millville Police credit her with making the Third Ward safer.

She and the principals of the school, including Bill Sheridan, who recently retired, were constantly working to brighten the lives, day by day, of the students. Often, her husband Greg, a talented craftsman with a big heart, has helped on projects ranging from building boats, to building jungle gyms, and everything in between. They never sought out credit or recognition, but they did receive it, as well they should. People like that seldom go unnoticed.

Recently, Gladis shared a very interesting story on how the political voting process occurred, not so long ago, in Millville's *Third Ward*. Gladis was just a kid at the time, but remembers it fondly and well:

"A lot of the polling places used to be in peoples' homes," she said. "We lived on Buck Street, and our voting station was located at Russell and Evelyn Bird's house on Foundry Street. They used to turn their living room into a voting parlor on election days. The front part of their house was a beauty shop. The business belonged to a very nice woman named Sarah Peterson. Women from all over the ward would go there to get their hair done and chit-chat about almost everything under the sun. I guess you could call it good-natured gossip.

"Evelyn Bird was on the Cumberland County election board. She and a handful of other people who were on the board would sign people in and monitor the voting. Somewhat similar to the way things are done today – but not quite. The big difference was that the ballots were counted by hand at the end of the day."

Gladis chuckled, and continued, "You sure couldn't get away with that today! This type of vote counting continued here in the *Third Ward* until the 1960's. Not sure if it was like that everywhere or not. All day long on Election Day, cars and trucks and people with bull horns would ride and walk around the streets, reminding the Third Warders to get out and vote. They would even hire some of the young men in the neighborhood on Election Day, those who had cars, to pick up senior citizens who couldn't get to a polling house. The young men would drive them there so they could cast their votes. Pretty nice thing to do, wasn't it?

"I remember that my grandmother had a habit of telling everyone she knew who she voted for. Oh my, she was such a proud, staunch Democrat. Every time grandmother announced who she was voting for, my mother would turn to us kids and say, 'now remember, you do not have to tell other people who you voted for. Voting in this country is a private privilege and you have a right to keep your vote to yourself. Do you kids understand that?' Mother would never tell us or anyone else who she voted for. Except for John F. Kennedy, that is. She told everybody that she voted for JFK. She was very proud of that vote. Good memories."

Gladis and her husband lived in the grand Victorian *Green House* on Columbia Avenue for 33 years. She moved out slightly more than a year ago. She said it has  been purchased by another single family. The house – admired by many as a prime example of Victorian structure – actually started out as a Colonial, said Gladis. She and her husband lovingly restored it. It has 23 *sleeping rooms*, which explained why it was used as a rooming house before the Mcgraws bought it. A little-known secret: The grand structure, with its unique turret, used to face the Maurice River before it was moved to its present site decades ago, Mcgraw said.

In 2000, Gladis helped form a grass-roots committee to help the *Third Ward* rise from the ashes. Sadly, many residents there felt the *Third Ward* hadn't seen any major improvements – not for a lack of trying by Gladis and other dedicated *Third Warders*. Authorities have praised Gladis for her tireless efforts to improve the neighborhood. She is a recipient of the *Pride in Millville Award* from the Chamber of Commerce.

The Sporting Life

The sports history of the *Third Ward* is chock full of heroes, villains, folklore and brutal truths. One constant has remained; *The Third Ward* and Millville at large have arguably produced as many talented and fascinating athletes as any other geographic region of its size in the United States. Some are well known, some not so well known.

City officials proudly presided over the dedication of Chiola Field in 1964.

Photo courtesy of Dale Wettstein

Millville football fields have produced the likes of *Bud MacAvoy* who scored touchdowns and made vicious tackles in the 1950s, and *Richie Panczyszyn*, the fleet-footed quarterback with the golden arm. Richie played on Millville's Wheaton field in the 1960s and later for Syracuse University. Amazingly, neither one of these two magical athletes ever played professionally.

Steve Romanik on the other hand, did make it to the professional ranks. Drafted in the third round by The Chicago Bears in 1950, Romanik played for Millville High from 1939 until 1942. After serving his country in the Army, Romanik suited up in college for the Villanova Wildcats. After an amazing career there, he was off to the big time, playing for the legendary coach, George Halas in

Chicago. After four years as quarterback of The Bears, and his final year as play caller and passer for the Chicago Cardinals (now the Phoenix Cardinals). Steve returned home to his beloved Millville.

Romanik's son, Jim, said, "My Dad grew up on Carmel Road, just across from the bluffs near Union Lake. He said that as a kid he would play in and around the lake, especially in the summer. He had a lot of friends in the *Third Ward*. There were a lot of good ball players that came out of there. Tough, ya know? Dad went to grammar school in the *Third Ward*. Wish he was still here so I could ask him."

Steve Romanik, a local icon, died in 2009. He served as City Commissioner of Parks and Public Property from 1965-1981.

John Lookabaugh, a gentle giant of a man, also played professional football. He grew up in West Virginia but moved to Millville after a successful he was drafted by the Washington Redskins in 1946. He played for them from 1946-1947. He co-owned and operated a painting business for the next 30 years in Millville. He painted many of the Victorian style houses and half-doubles in the Third Ward. His son John remembers that "Dad was painting the steeple of The West Side Church. He fell off the roof and broke two fingers. But that didn't stop him from building his business up and continue painting. My Dad was a very nice man, very humble. The only person he ever yelled at was me," he added with a smile.

Larry Milbourne, a 1969 Millville High graduate played Major League Baseball for numerous teams in both the American and National leagues. *Alan Shaw*, the 6'11" basketball player, carried Millville to the final round of the state basketball playoffs, also in 1969. Although technically not a Third Warder, he was integral to the team. Millville lost to Perth Amboy in that nail-biting final game held at the Atlantic City Convention Center. Shaw later played for Duke University and professionally in Europe.

There are many, many more sparkling athletes who were born and raised in Millville, all of whom either lived in the Third Ward or had close ties there. It seems utterly impossible to have grown up anywhere in Millville, New Jersey or attended Millville High School without being affected by the colorful character of *"The Bloody Third Ward."*

Mike Trout

Now to the present: Whether you're a baseball fan or not, you have to have been living under a rock the past few years not to have heard the name *Mike Trout*. Considered the best player in the sport today – if not ever – the young man from Millville has become somewhat of a phenomenon. It seems he can do anything. Trout is the baseball center fielder for the *Los Angeles Angels* of Anaheim of *Major League Baseball* (MLB). He is an *American League* (AL) *Most Valuable Player* (MVP) award nominee, placing 2nd two years running, and three-time *All-Star* since becoming a regular player in 2012.

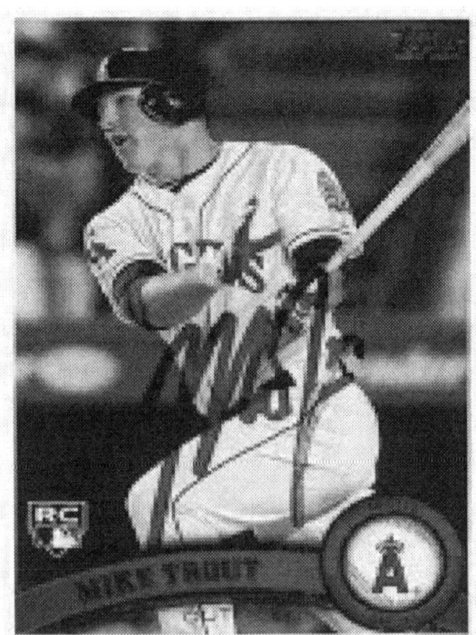

*Considered by many to be the best baseball player in
the Major Leagues today (and perhaps of all time) is
Millville's Mike Trout. His great-grandfather John "Bat" Trout
played baseball, for the Whitall-Tatum company decades ago.*
Photo courtesy of the Trout family

Millville's Mike Trout is considered by many to be the best baseball player in the Major Leagues today. Others claim Mike is perhaps the best player of all time. Trout was a first round pick by the Angels in the 2009 MLB draft, and made a brief major league appearance in 2011. A year later, he went on to win the 2012 Rookie of the Year Award.

Trout finished second in the American League's Most Valuable Player voting in 2012 and again 2013, before winning the 2014 American League All-Star Game MVP Award and the 2014 American League Hank Aaron Award. Mike won his second straight All-Star Game MVP award in 2015, something never done before. Not surprisingly, his family has baseball roots in the Third Ward.

Nelson Trout, Mike's uncle, recalled the early years of his nephew's baseball *career*:

"I remember pitching Wiffle balls to Mike when he was just a little boy. You could tell he was special, even then. One day on the beach in Strathmere, (a New Jersey beach) when Mike was about five-years-old, we all forgot to bring the Wiffle ball bat to the beach. Mike, as usual, wanted to bat balls into the ocean that day. When he realized we didn't have the bat that either his dad or I would always bring to the beach, he took off walking down the shoreline. We kept an eye on him as he bent over and picked up a piece of driftwood. When he brought it back, he took a couple of practice swings with the driftwood, using it as his makeshift baseball bat. Then, he looked at his dad and me and said, 'I'm ready to hit now.'"

"I'll never forget that," his uncle said with a smile.

Mike Trout has an interesting connection to the *Third Ward*.

Mike's great-grandfather, *John "Bat" Trout*, was also a well-known slugger in his day. He was a star on the Whitall Tatum company baseball team in the 1930s.

The team was comprised mostly of hard-working Third Warders wishing to relieve the stress of the monotonous factory work. *"Bat" Trout* was more than happy to join them in playing baseball for his boss, George Bacon who was the superintendent of Whitall Tatum.

Bacon lived in one of the few *mansions* in the *Third Ward* inhabited by industrial leaders. The workers in his plants mostly came from the more modest *Third Ward* neighborhoods.

"Bat" Trout quickly became locally famous for *hittin' em in the river,* and for his hot temper – the river being the Maurice River, which runs down through Millville from Union lake. The river is situated deep over the left field fence and across the road from Chiola Field, a long way from home plate. Chiola Field was where Whitall Tatum took on all their challengers, usually beating them decisively and *"Bat" Trout* was the main attraction.

Dedication Ceremony for Chiola Field:
"Bat" Trout was famous for hittin' em in the river from Chiola Field

Trout made his living in the glass factory's *hot end*, where the sand was melted, and the glass was made. Whitall Tatum, of course, was one of the largest employers in the area at the time, and located in the heart of Millville's *Third Ward. "Bat" Trout* also played on semi-pro baseball teams throughout the South Jersey area, where his reputation as a power hitter was, and still is, legendary.

"Bat" Trout's grandson, Mike Trout's father, Jeff Trout, was drafted by the Minnesota Twins in 1984.Jeff was selected as the first-team All American Second Baseman after a stellar career at the University of Delaware. Jeff still holds batting records at Millville High School and the University of Delaware.

The Bloody Third
By: Eileen Bennett & Nelson Trout

Mike Trout's father, Jeff Trout, was drafted by the Minnesota Twins in 1984. Also in 1984, Jeff was selected as the first-team All American Second Baseman after a stellar career at the University of Delaware.
Photo courtesy of the Trout family.

His son Mike is the 2014 and the 2015 Most Valuable Player of the Major League All-Star Games, the only person to win that award two years in a row as well as the 2014 winner of the Hank Aaron Award.

Mike's great grandfather, John "Bat" Trout, the flamboyant third ward baseball star of yesterday, would surely be bursting with pride at young Mike's astounding accomplishments.

Coach Ed Andrews

Well-known and beloved Millville High school football and baseball coach Ed Andrews, 71, was himself born and raised in four different homes in Millville's Third Ward. Andrews was also a physical education teacher who taught generations of Millville athletes, including many from *The Bloody Third*. Today, Andrews points to his childhood in the Third Ward as part of his success.

His story of growing up in *The Bloody Third* is typical of many young men of his generation. He remembers his *Third Ward* neighborhoods as *rough and tough,* and consisting of mostly factory workers, either in one of the city's two glass houses, Wheaton Glass and Armstrong Cork, or the Cotton Mill.

Sports for the kids in that era consisted of the neighborhood boys playing whichever sport was in season. This included tackle football in the streets, some paved, some gravel. It made for brutal contact not only with each other, but with the hard, unforgiving streets. There were no helmets, shoulder pads or knee pads.

"That's how we played back then," Coach Andrews said, laughing. "It made us tough and some of the best football players ever to come out of Millville High inherited their toughness from those pick-up games on the mean streets of the *Bloody Third Ward.*" It's no surprise that many fine athletes hailed from the *Bloody Third.* There were no fancy ballparks. The boys from the *Third Ward* were known as scrappers who learned sports the hard way.

Andrews – known to generations of Millvillians simply as "Coach" – was born on Oct. 27, 1943 to Allen Jr. and Irene Andrews at 404 Powell Street and lived there until the age of 6. They had no hot water. "I was potty trained in an outhouse. My mother would heat hot water on the stove and pour it into the bath tub once a week to give us kids a bath," Coach said.

The family moved to High and McNeal streets from 1950 until 1952, across the street from the old Whitaker's ice plant. He and his friends often played in the *tunnel* which ran under High Street from McNeal Street to the ice plant. It was sometime during these two years that the Andrews family purchased their first television set. They paid for it *on time* from the now long gone Firestone store on High Street.

"Kids from the neighborhood would come over to gather around our TV. Most of the families in that section of the Third Ward didn't have televisions yet," he said.

Toward the end of 1952, the Andrews family moved yet again – this time to 404 Foundry Street, just off of Church Street. The house was owned by attorney Santo Salvo. Conveniently, for his father, it was located right next door to the *Third Ward Tavern.*

Looking back, Andrews said he believes his father was a functional alcoholic – again, not uncommon during those hard-working days in Millville's scrappy *Third Ward*. Andrews however, seldom missed work, and his main focus in life was providing for his family.

"I guess we were kind of poor, but didn't know it," the good-natured coach said with a smile.

Interestingly, behind what are now the Child Family Center and the Andrews' back yard, was a huge horse corral.

"The horses ran free and loose within the confines of the corral. We used to pet them and swing on the squeaky gate of the corral. Yep, horses right in the center of town!" the Coach said, laughing. "It's a lot different now. Near the horse corral, there were also these high big piles of coal. We used to get filthy playing on them, running up and down those coal hills."

Coach Andrews also played organized baseball during the very first year that Little League Baseball arrived in the Holly City. This was sometime during the early '50s. "I went to Saint Mary's School through grammar school, which was right next door to R.D. Wood School. I remember having snowball fights – Saint Mary's School against Wood School. Man that was fun, just good natured fun! We had a ball!"

On the move once again, the family of five moved to Dock Street at Oak Street. By this time young Ed was suited up in a Millville High School football uniform.

"It really took some getting used to. I mean, it was the first time I ever played football on a field of mowed grass with a helmet and shoulder pads. It was the same for all of us guys coming out of the *Third Ward*, but we were (laughing again) a tough bunch and our coaches recognized that right away. One of the *Third Ward* guys who became a star quarterback for Millville High was my best friend Jimmy Smith. But most of us were just hard-nosed, unheralded players, which through the years – and until this very day – our football teams are well known for around the state."

Not surprisingly, football would be Andrew's eventual ticket out of the storied *Third Ward* and on to an exciting new life. He would become the first member of his family to attend college, and his gridiron abilities helped him get there. Accepted by both Salem College in Salem, West Virginia. and Springfield College in Massachusetts, the future Millville High School football coach chose Salem College. Up until that time "the furthest west I had ever been was Bridgeton."

Because his parents never owned a car, he was driven to college by the parents of his pretty high school sweetheart, Bonnie, captain of the MHS cheerleaders. They would marry and just celebrated their 50th wedding anniversary in August 2015.

While in college not only did Ed have a distinguished football career, but was also a member of the Doo-Wap singing group called *The Loungeman.*

"The singing was fun, but I never expected to make a career of it," Andrews said, once again grinning at the memory. After graduating from college, he returned to his hometown to teach physical education and coach football at Millville High School under legendary head coach Tony Surace. It is through the eyes of Ed Andrews that we can observe what life was like growing up in the *Bloody Third Ward* and how it helped to develop his strong and caring character. Over the years, he passed these virtues down to hundreds of athletes.

The Rivalry

Ed Andrews played stellar football for Millville High School for four years. His first year, as a freshman, he was invited to suit up and watch the Thanksgiving Day game between Millville and neighboring Vineland with the varsity team from the sidelines. The Millville vs. Vineland Thanksgiving Day Classic began in 1894 and is the 12th oldest rivalry of its kind in the United States.

"Wow! What an honor for a kid like me, who just a couple of years ago was playing tackle football on the infamous streets of *The Bloody Third*, in the shadows of the Cotton Mill and the Third Ward Tavern," Andrews said.

He, along with the other selected freshman were to be witnesses to one of the biggest high school football rivalries in the country – *The Millville-Vineland Thanksgiving Day Classic,* which continues to this day. This event was so colossal that several thousand fans packed the stands and stood 10 and 20 deep around the perimeter of the field. Standing room only was a feeble understatement when these two powerhouses went head-to-head every Thanksgiving day for more than a century. Police, some with trained riot dogs and helmets patrolled the complex to prevent and break up fights that would inevitably break out during this emotionally- charged, momentous battle on the field. Whether the game was held in Millville on Wheaton Field or at Gittone Stadium in Vineland, the players held the heart, soul and pride of their respective cities in their hands that day. They realized what an honor it was to be one of the gifted and fortunate 22 modern day gladiators playing to the deafening cheers and jeers of the countless generations of frenzied fans and how the outcome would affect not only their turkey dinners later in the day, but the bragging rights, which meant everything for the following year.

"We players were well aware of that. We were all bursting with pride," Andrews recalled.

The Bloody Third
By: Eileen Bennett & Nelson Trout

Without a doubt, the Thanksgiving Day Classic between Millville and Vineland was and still is the absolute pinnacle of High School football rivalries.

Home for the holidays during his first year at Salem College, Ed Andrews and his girlfriend Bonnie attended the Turkey Day Classic, which that year was held at Gittone Stadium in Vineland. For the first time in five years he would be a spectator instead of a player, and Bonnie would be just another pretty face in the crowd instead cheering on the players.

"It really felt strange watching the game from the stands, but I could still feel the excitement that I knew the players were experiencing," Andrews recalled. They went to the game in holiday spirit with another couple, Gary Kline and Christine White. Ed wore his *Group 3* championship jacket which Millville had earned the year before when Ed played as a senior, and Bonnie led the crowd in cheers from the sidelines. "I was and still am, very proud of that jacket," he said.

It was a close game right up until the very end when freshman Richie Panczyszyn threw a touchdown pass to win the game for Millville in the final seconds of the nail-biting showdown. "Panzy," one of South Jersey's all-time best athletes, later received a full football scholarship to Syracuse University.

"Bonnie and I were hoarse from cheering, nearly jumping out of the stands when Panzy threw that touchdown pass!" Andrews recalled. Another classic was registered in the history books as a Millville win. As the final whistle blew, Ed told Bonnie, Gary and Christine, "I'll be right back. I'm going down on the field to congratulate the team." They excitingly replied, "Okay Ed, we'll meet you back at the car" which was parked on Landis Avenue in front of the Vineland High School. The field was situated behind the school. He was unprepared for what was going to happy next.

"On my way back to the car, walking alone with my championship Millville jacket on, I was jumped and pummeled, at first on the back of the head, by a group of disgruntled Vineland fans," Andrews said. "Then came the body and face punches. Trying to escape the beating, I took off running up Landis Avenue to a group of Millville guys I spotted through the blur of punches coming at me like a swarm of killer bees." When he reached his buddies, some were, like Ed, former Millville football players, a crowd formed around the gang fight. The police arrived shouting orders and drawing billy clubs, seemingly settling things down. But another fight broke out, then another. The cops, themselves obviously rattled, began hitting some of the brawlers with their clubs. One of the guys, who jumped in to help his buddy and former teammate, fighting side-by-side to fend off the attackers, was Rob Shannon, who would later become the mayor of Millville. Andrews recalls Shannon being hit by the police and thrown on top of a squad car, all the while trying to explain to the police that they did not start the fight, but were obviously ready to finish it in grand Millville style. "We were subdued and whisked away to the Vineland Police Station, where Rob was officially arrested, which was really unfair because, like I said, we didn't start the fight."

Bonnie, Gary and Christine happened to glimpse Bonnie's future husband, along with his buddy Rob in the back seat of a police car on their way to the station. The crowd they had drawn was still large, and the remaining policeman finally dispersed them with a little help from their canine comrades. Amazingly, no one was seriously injured. Episodes such as this were almost typical when Millville and Vineland engaged in their annual "Clash of the Titans"

Andrews recalled that Rob Shannon called his father, owner of the prestigious Rocap-Shannon funeral home in Millville and asked him to come pick him and Ed up at the Vineland police headquarters.

Mr. Shannon, showing a degree of tough love said, "No, you got yourself into this, now get yourself out," and promptly hung up the phone.

Since Andrews's parents never owned a car there was no chance of them bailing the pair out.

Eventually they phoned a mutual friend named John Trainer who drove to Vineland and brought the dynamic duo home to Millville.

The Infamous 'Walk Out'

Through the years there have been a myriad of teachers and coaches who have endeared themselves to the athletes they coached and students they taught at their beloved Millville Senior High School, without a doubt, far too many to mention. One of those favorite teacher/coaches however, sparked an unprecedented show of love and support which culminated into the only walk-out in the fascinating history of the school, home of The Millville Thunderbolts. It was in the spring of 1972.

"That's the time of year when the Board of Education, at that time appointed by the Millville City Commission, would announce which teachers would be rehired for the following school year as well as those who would not," Andrews explained.

Swinging the night away at a YMCA dance.

Photo courtesy of Dale Wettstein

That year the School Board made the surprising announcement that physical education teacher and coach, Ed

Andrews, who was not yet under tenure, along with six of his colleagues would not be rehired for the next year. "We were shocked, blindsided," Andrews said. A simple philosophical disagreement between Andrews and the school board president was apparently the reason for this decision, which to this day appears to be baseless other than the fact that the board president evidently did not like the fact that a young popular teacher and coach would stick to his guns and have the moxie to express his difference of opinion with the powerful president.

"As far as I was concerned, the two of us would simply agree to disagree and move on in adult fashion with the best interest of the student body at heart," Andrews said. But that's not quite what happened, and Andrews, along with the other six young educators, were not rehired.

The news spread rapidly through the hallways of Millville Senior High. The fire, fanned by the dedication and admiration the students felt for Coach Andrews also spread quickly across the entire town. Not only his saddened and furious pupils, but their parents and the citizenry at large were at first dumfounded and then outraged by this groundless decision.

An impressive group of Millville High students gathered and decided that the one thing that would grab the attention of the board and punctuate how important and wrong they thought the decision to fire Andrews would be was to stage a "walk-out."

"Hey, we just wouldn't go to school until Coach Andrews was rehired. It was that simple," recalled Tim Shannon who recently commented on the historic action taken over those next ten days.

"Those kids really touched my heart. I was totally surprised and humbled by that."

The leaders of the civil disobedience protest consisted of Shannon, Chuck Lore, Kevin Trout and Dave Sharpless, just to name a few. Sharpless himself would later become a popular teacher and football coach at Millville High. The group and their cause not only had a huge following of fellow students and fans of Andrews, but their parents, city commissioners, who had ironically appointed the school board members, along with Lew Finch, a powerful behind-the-scenes political force at the time as well as the director of the all-important Millville Airport. Strategy meetings were held in the popular Red Cottage luncheonette, located on the corner of Fourth and Sassafras streets, owned by former Millville High School football player, Rocco "Rocky' Biggs.

"I kind of stayed in the background while all of this was going on and let them run with the ball. Very grateful, because I had a young family to support, and I loved my job. I needed my job!" Coach Andrews said.

A rally was even held at one point in the Millville Senior High School auditorium to an overflow crowd which spilled out to the parking lots on both sides of the adjacent wide hallways outside the auditorium. The huge room erupted into a thunderous roar as Andrews was called to the stage.

"I was holding back the tears that night, let me tell ya." Without even trying, Andrews had assembled a formidable force whose common goal was to keep the popular young mentor in Millville as a coach and educator. The group even had the support of the chief of police, Charles Pangburn who issued the group a bullhorn in the name of safety. With the bullhorn, the leaders could communicate with the long line of supporters who marched from school to school announcing the folly of the board's decision and their efforts to have that decision overturned. One spring day the now-huge group of Andrews's supporters carried a symbolic casket from the Senior High School on Wade Boulevard, down Broad Street past the Junior High School. From there, the marchers turned left on High Street where the Board of Education offices were located, onward past City Hall, down the famous City Hall Hill to Chiola Field, overlooking the Maurice River. It was there that a large rally was held for the worthy cause of reinstating Andrews as well as the other six teachers who had been dismissed by the board.

"When I heard about that, the casket march and all, I was really blown away, and so was Bonnie," Coach Andrews recalled.

Eventually, after roughly ten days of near-empty classrooms, extensive local and Philadelphia news coverage and the emergency appointment of three new Board of Education members, the decision was reversed. The beloved and now famous, Coach Ed Andrews, that little boy who was potty-trained in an outhouse in *The Bloody Third Ward* of Millville, had won back his job. The other six teachers, on Andrew's coattails, were also reinstated, although one of the six had already taken a job in another school district, he would later return to Millville Senior High school as an administrator.

Interior of Jim's Lunch, unknown date. This long-standing
Restaurant remains one of the most popular eateries in the city.
Strategy sessions were held here during the walkout.

Photo courtesy of Dale Wettstein

"What a bunch of kids," Andrews recalled. "I mean they got the whole town involved, and to this day I am and will forever be extremely grateful.

Today Coach Ed Andrews is retired and lives in Millville with his still-lovely childhood sweetheart, Bonnie.

Folklore

Without a doubt, the most incredible legend in the state of New Jersey is the spine-tingling tale of *The Jersey Devil*. Although there are several versions of this strange New Jersey canard, it seems that the most accepted theory is that the *unusual* creature, which is also referred to as *The Leeds Devil* roams the woods, and sometimes the streets of southern New Jersey. The *Third Ward* of Millville was no exception.

The Devil has reportedly been spotted almost everywhere in the state and was supposedly born in the Pine Barrens, somewhere in Atlantic County, N.J. to the unfortunate Deborah Leeds. The Pine Barrens spreads across seventeen hundred square miles of southeastern New Jersey and is known for its nearly uninhabitable landscape, iron and cedar stained streams and dwarf pine trees. The soil, unlike much of the Garden State is very sandy and not conducive to farming. The few people who lived in the Pine Barrens, especially in the mid-1700s, when Mrs. Leeds gave birth to the ill-fated child, were poor, uneducated and somewhat isolated from the rest of New Jersey and indeed, the world. Alas, her thirteenth child would bring, if not fame, infamy to the region, however, in a most frightening manner.

Fable has it that the *Jersey Devil* was the thirteenth child born to Deborah Leeds and her husband, Japhet Leeds. Deborah was not happy with the idea of another child, as the family was already destitute and impoverished, typical of the scattered families in the Pine Barrens at the time. Just before the baby was born with the help of a midwife whom Mr. Leeds had brought to the cabin, Deborah screamed out, "Let this child be a devil, I am tired of children at my feet"! As the midwife brought the child from Deborah's womb it appeared normal and much resembled the first dozen Leeds children at birth.

Less than an hour later as the newborn lay in the exhausted arms of sad Mother Leeds, a morbid transformation took place as a raging storm battered the outer walls of the cramped cabin. The newest member of the Leeds family began to grow and morph before the horrified eyes of the midwife and the rest of the Leeds family.

The baby's body grew into an elongated creature of between three and four feet in length. The human features dissolved into the unspeakable shape of a reptilian beast with the wings of a bat, the head of a serpent and the pointed tale of a gargoyle. It is then that the devil-baby flew out of Mary's arms and around the room before beating the midwife to death with its powerful wings. The thirteenth and apparently cursed child then thinned its body and with a terrifying screech, rumored to have been heard throughout the Pine Barrens for miles, flew up the chimney and was never seen again by Deborah Leeds, her husband or the twelve remaining siblings who were frozen in fear at the unbelievable sight.

Since then, there have been hundreds if not thousands of people from all walks of life who swear they have seen and even been attacked by the *Jersey Devil*. Numerous encounters, mostly visual, have been reported in Millville, especially in the Union Lake area of the city. This area is heavily wooded and rubs elbows with *The Bloody Third Ward*. The Maurice River which flows out of Union Lake runs through the heart of the *Third Ward* and was used to power the Cotton Mill for many decades.

There was a spate of *Jersey Devil* sightings in the Vineland-Millville area during the 1950s and 1960s, when the poultry industry was booming, particularly in Vineland. Farmers said in the mornings, they would find their chickens dead – with no visible sign of an attack. They blamed the *Jersey Devil.*

Every old time seems to have a spooky legend attached to it. *The Third Ward* is no exception.

Below is just one of a number of reported visual accounts of the infamous *Jersey Devil* in Millville's *Bloody Third Ward* – and beyond – over the years, by Millville resident George Romer, in his own words:

"I've seen your posts on Facebook and have been reluctant to reach out because of the absurdity of my story," he wrote. "My early years were spent growing up in the *Third Ward* and I attended R.D. Wood School from kindergarten all the way through sixth grade.

"It was a rough neighborhood, but spats always eventually resulted in making amends and playing ball together by the next day. No stabbings or shootings which prevail today. We lived in the area of Archer and McNeal streets and spent many hours at Union Lake, canal and cotton mill areas. They were our playgrounds. My first friend was, and still is today, John Martin. We remained friends all through high school and right into the seventies, which brings me closer to my story.

"He was born and raised in the *Third Ward* and remained there until he moved to Texas. He and I would often sit in his living room watching the late movie, and the late, late movie on a weekend night (the one that had a big clock displayed and the catchy tune.... da dunt dunt dunt dunt da dada dada da). We loved watching the thrillers and scary movies like, "The Mummy," "Dracula," "Werewolf," "Swamp Thing," "Godzilla," "Monthra," etc. His house was right across from Arlene Village apartments located on Archer, Foundry streets and Arnold Drive.

"It was a warm summer night in the early nineteen seventies – or I should say early morning? It was after midnight. We were in his living room; the front window was open because most families could not afford an air conditioner back then. We were really engrossed in one of those old movies. I forgot to mention – it was the night before trash pickup and most of the folks in the neighborhood had already put their galvanized cans to the curb for the next day's pickup. Both of us simultaneously heard a loud whoosh, some rustling and a slight clanging outside of the window by the curb.

"We both immediately looked at each other and then leaned over to the window to see what was causing the noise. I still recall it clearly.....perched there on top of one of the opened cans was a creature about four-and-a-half to five feet in height, with large wings, a scaly looking head with a large beak, scaly legs and a reptile like tail about three foot long. It had huge piercing eyes that were peering right at us. It only stayed for a second after it saw us looking at it; and then it leaped with a blood curdling scream, knocking over the can and strewing trash into the street and flew off into the dark of Arlene Village with just a few flaps of its wings. We sat for quite a while, looking back and forth at each other and at the curb without saying a word for the rest of the night."

The Bloody Third

By: Eileen Bennett & Nelson Trout

There is another beastly creature that many in southern New Jersey say roams the wooded areas, terrifying anyone who happens to catch a glimpse of it. This strange curiosity is known as *Lamb Legs*. Infamous for its half-man, half-lamb body, *Lamb Legs* is reported as a frightful and solitary character that travels with great speed and agility among the pines and oaks on the outskirts of Millville. Dashing in and out of the moonlight, the monster often sounds a tormented scream as it vanishes into the night. Others have recalled that *Lamb Legs* is silent and stealthy, sneaking up on people almost without a sound. Never has it been captured or photographed, although many have tried.

Most accounts of *Lamb Legs* seem to be in the late 1960s and early 1970s, although there are still periodic glimpses of him reported. It is recalled that teenagers, many from Millville's *Third Ward*, would courageously venture into the thickets and brush in pursuit of the bedeviled anomaly. Most sightings were in an area nicknamed "*The Monster Farm*," which lies at the end of Leamings Mill Road, over the bridge and left down a dirt road leading off into the woods, a few miles east of downtown Millville. A successful local businessman, whom we'll call JT, used to camp out in the surrounding wilderness of Millville as a teenager and young adult. He shared a spine-tingling encounter he had with *Lamb Legs* in 1974.

JT explained in his own words:

"Me and two other guys were near the bank of the little pond on the south side of Leamings Mill Bridge. I was making a sandwich, sitting next to the camp fire that my buddies and I had built, I'd say about twenty or thirty feet up the bank. I was the only one at the fire because they were night fishing with a lantern down on shore. It was probably around ten or eleven o'clock on a Saturday night. Maybe a little later. My back was to the deeper side of the woods so I could watch the other two guys fish," he added. "At first I thought I heard a squirrel bouncing around behind me because I could hear some pine needles and oak leaves crunch. Then the noise stopped for a few seconds so I didn't pay much attention to it. Then I could hear what sounded like a deer walking up close behind me, and I got a weird feeling, like I was being watched. I turned my head around and less than a yard from me was the craziest thing I ever saw. There was a man's face with a beard that looked wet, and it shined from the fire. The bottom of the guy looked really strange but I was locked in on his eyes. He looked very upset. After like, five seconds or even less, he ran back into the woods. I saw the back of his legs then, and I instantly thought it looked like the back of a small horse or a pony. I screamed and my buddies ran up the bank. I told them what I saw, exactly! They looked around with the lantern, but I was too scared to move. We had all heard about *Lamb Legs* for many years, but no way thought it could be real. The horse legs I thought I saw could easily have been the legs of a pretty big lamb. We couldn't believe it, but I think I saw *Lamb Legs*. I'll never forget that night as long as I live."

Lamb Legs has also been frequently spotted at another well-known teenage party spot known as *Tavern Rock*. Tavern Rock is likewise deep in the sylvan, a few miles south, if traveling through the woods, of Monster Farm. You can also reach Tavern Rock by driving east of Millville on route 49 and making a left hand turn down a dirt road just before the Holly Farm. The Holly Farm, famous for its acres of huge and healthy holly trees, is on the opposite side of the road just west of the Menantico sand wash area. The undisturbed ponds and woodlands around Menantico are, to this day, very popular with fisherman and hunters. Speculation has it that *Lamb Legs* has for decades traveled nightly between the Monster Farm and Tavern Rock, sleeping obscurely during the day.

Legend has it that *Lamb Legs* was a normal man at one time. The man had his legs severed in a horrible industrial accident and a mysterious doctor repaired him by attaching a set of legs from a large lamb to the man's torso. Some people believe that *Lamb Legs* may even be an offspring of *The Jersey Devil*, while others discount that notion for a variety of reasons. So many people with fine reputations have come forward through the years to solemnly and soberly share their experiences of encountering *Lamb Legs* that one can only assume that something is going on between the Monster Farm and Tavern Rock. Perhaps someday someone will get a picture of whatever or whoever roams that pristine section of forest on the fringes of Millville.

Millville resident Earl Gramlich has a more down-to-earth explanation for the local spooky legends.

"First, Tavern Rock is located off Route 49 on a road that angles to the left just before going up the hill that the Holly Farm entrance is. The road now leads to the Whitehead property, although that is a left turn into the road whereas to get to Tavern Rock was a straight in route on the road.

"From what my dad told me – and we actually small-game hunted back there – it was an old sand mining place, kind of like Menantico (sand plant) but a different kind of sand. There used to be tunnels through the white sand area that I actually crawled through in my younger days. I suppose it is all caved in by now, but at one time it was an awesome place for kids to go to, especially at night.

"As I grew old enough to drive and go back there, there were occult things happening as well, although I can't back that up; but I can tell you that one night, as I took one of the many entrances into the area...to go parking...there was a chicken hanging in the roadway."

Gramlich also expounded on the *Monster Farm* legend.

"Now as for the *Monster farm*, that is located at the end of Leamings Mill Road, just over the bridge to the left. It was blocked off years ago so I'm sure entry is still not there. If you go over that little bridge, you'll see a house up, and to your left. It was actually an old abandoned Christmas tree farm, so you can just imagine the scene at night, with all those overgrown various species of pine trees waving in the night breeze. Also, remember, this was a time when hallucinogens were very popular. The kids would go back there to party. It is said (and I have never seen this as I didn't go back there during the drug use) but supposedly, the current owner of the house that you see upon your left turn into the area, wanted to rid the alcohol/drug parties that continued to go on every weekend, so he started to dress up as some kind of *Demon/Monster*, and scare the hell out of the kids that were back there partying. Supposedly, this wasn't hard for him to do, since most were already under the influence of something that altered their minds."

"You know," Gramlich added, "I'm wondering if this '*Lamb Legs*' thing isn't tied into the monster farm. And those who grew up in the Millville, Cumberland County area in the 1970s or earlier may recall daring friends to venture into the woods at night in search of "*Lamb Legs*," a half-man, half-lamb horror" on the Internet. It sounds exactly like what kids were doing back there – going back there to party and see the "*monster*."

The legend of *"Lamb Legs"* prompts another subject about which a few *Third Warders* offer up myths of the unknown: Unidentified Flying Objects sighted in their community. They weren't alone. As a matter of fact, many celebrities openly speak of their encounters with UFOs.

President Jimmy Carter, Mick Jagger, Jackie Gleason, Billy Ray Cyrus, John Lennon, Ronald Reagan, Muhammad Ali, David Bowie, Will Smith, Alexander the Great, Dan Akroyd, Lech Walesa, Christopher Columbus, Russell Crowe, Dennis Kucinich, and Millville residents, Linda Morgan, Douglas Larosa and Diane Renee Howard Kuppel all have each publically claimed that they have seen at least one unidentified flying object in their lifetime – UFOs.

There have been, and continue to be, millions of UFO sightings reported every year across our country and the world. Policeman, airline pilots, air traffic controllers, astronauts, not to mention average, everyday citizens have all stood fast in their conviction that they have seen something from outside our planet in the skies, and yes, even on the ground. Experts in this field believe that most sightings go unreported, adding to the body of evidence that something is going on that not even the most brilliant scientists can fully explain.

On Aug. 27, 1952, Linda Morgan and her family were celebrating her grandmother's fiftieth birthday in one of the beautiful cottages, which at the time were located on the eastern shore of Union Lake in Millville – Cottage Number 5 to be exact. The family was in the living room in the center of the cottage when they heard some neighbors from a few of the other cottages calling for them to come out and see what was slowly flying across the top of the Union Lake dam.

Linda recalls that, "We all went out to the screened in porch that hung out over the lake to see what all the commotion was. When we got there, a number of our neighbors were pointing south toward the dam, saying 'Look, look, what is it, I can't believe how big it is!' We all stood out on the porch and saw this huge round object in the sky, right above the dam. It reminded me of a giant tambourine. It had lights all around the outside of it that were blinking on and off. They looked kind of yellowish. The object was kind of dark gray in color, almost black. I think we were all in what you would call a state of shock at first, and honestly could not believe that what we were seeing was real. But it was, because it was there for about ten minutes, moving slowly, like a blimp, toward the bluffs on the other side of the lake. Finally, it just disappeared off into the sky, moving west. None of us will ever forget that night, it was just before dark, and we still talk about it quite a bit. A lot of people saw the thing; it was very visible all across the *Third Ward*. I'm sure a lot of other people saw it. I mean, how could they miss it?"

On a clear summer night in 1975, Douglas Larosa, a devout Christian and heavy equipment operator for his father's construction business, was camping out with some friends in the woods that encircle Union Lake. The sky was clear. Hot dogs and marshmallows were sizzling over an open camp fire. It was a little past midnight and the close-knit group of friends was getting ready to bed down until morning as soon as they finished their last snack of the night. After all, fishing in the morning was on the menu and they would need to be fresh with energy. Hard workers by day and nature lovers by night, the group had camped out here, on the edge of Millville's third ward, many times, both as kids and now, as young adults.

One of the young men thought he saw something move across the moon, which was not quite, but almost, full that night. At first he was quiet and, "He just kept staring up," Larosa recalled.

The others asked him what he was looking at. He pointed up to where the moon had been.

Douglas energetically recalls that mystical moment, when: "The other guys and I looked up and couldn't really comprehend what we were seeing right away. There was this enormous round thing that covered almost the whole lake, just sitting there in the sky, not making any kind of sound at all. It wasn't even that high off the lake and was all black- barely moving at all.

"Like I said, it was low in the sky, just a little bit above the tree tops on the little island over near where the boat ramp is now, at the bottom of the bluffs. Nobody said anything, but I remember one of the guys, I think it was Andy, grabbing my arm. The moon was gone, we couldn't see the moon. All of a sudden all of these lights started blinking around the outside of it, and you could see the outline of the thing. I swear, it was almost as big as the lake. The lights were kind of yellow with some red ones every few feet or so, but mostly kind of yellow.

"I think we all wanted to run, but we were literally frozen and couldn't take our eyes off of it and couldn't talk. It was really scary, but more than that, I felt like my whole world had just changed. Nothing made sense anymore, but everything suddenly did. It's hard to explain. I knew it wasn't from here. Sorry, I'm shivering. I always do when I talk about that night – which isn't very often.

"From the middle of the bottom of it, a bright light like a spot light shined down on the lake. It was so bright that it lit up almost the whole lake.

"I never took my eyes off of it. I knew my flashlight was right next to me, so I felt around for it and found it. I pointed it up at the thing, and about a minute later, like a flash, it was gone.

"At first, after it had been gone for a few minutes, we wanted to go tell everybody we could find about it. I mean, it was so amazing and life changing, I can't tell you. But after we talked about it (one of the guys started crying and wouldn't stop) and thought about it, we decided not to tell anybody – unless somebody else had seen it, or if it was in the papers or on the news, or something. Then we would come forward. But it wasn't in any newspapers or on the news, so we kept it to ourselves for quite a few years. The first person I told was my wife. At first she thought I was kidding. I wasn't." The "*Union Lake sighting*" has been a story handed down through the years.

The above tales are typical of much of the folklore that has encircled the lake and the surrounding area since its early days. A variety of activities take place throughout the year for children and adults who are drawn to the peacefulness of a quiet walk, or to the more energetic activity of youth. And as any place of natural beauty, Union Lake Park has provided the background for pictures to record the event for posterity.

*The Women's Christian Temperance Union
holding a "beauty contest" at Union Lake Park.*

Photo courtesy of Dale Wettstein

The Haunting of Carrie Wood

It can be argued that the City of Millville may not exist today without the entrepreneurship of the Wood family. The family's impact can even be felt today. Many people don't realize that without the Wood family, there wouldn't be any of the ubiquitous Wawa convenience stores that dot main thoroughfares on the East Coast.

Richard Davis Wood built the cotton mill and financed the creation of Union Lake, which supplied power to the mill. In later years, his family was the founder of the Wawa Corporation, which has stores in New Jersey, Pennsylvania, Delaware, Maryland, Virginia and Florida.

The Wood family lived at 821 Columbia Avenue, which is still referred to as the *"Wood Mansion."* The house was built in 1814 and was built for Wood's beloved daughter, Caroline, or *"Carrie,"* as she was known.

The Bloody Third
By: Eileen Bennett & Nelson Trout

Portrait of heiress Carrie Wood, circa 1800.

Photo courtesy of Greg Geraci

Initially she didn't care for the house, preferring the wide open fields of Pennsylvania. But she grew to love the house so much, she never wanted to leave it.

Carrie, daughter of Richard and Juliana Wood, was thrown from a horse and killed in 1857, at the age of nineteen. She had been riding in Westchester County, Pennsylvania, near Wawa, Pa., on the family farm at the time of her death. Nonetheless, some say she still haunts the rooms of the historic *Wood Mansion* in Millville.

Carrie spent a lot of her young life in Millville's *Third Ward* with her parents, Richard and Juliana Wood. Bob Francois of the Millville Historical Society points out the interesting fact:

"Carrie kept a diary, and at first, she didn't like the Millville house on Columbia Avenue very much at all. She complained that the house had no shade, no large porches and there was no grass growing in the yard at the time. Carrie changed her mind about the house though, and fell in love with the large, beautiful rooms.

"She enjoyed spending time in Millville with her parents, and a couple of years after Carrie died, porches were added and landscaping was done on the property," Francois said.

It seems that for as far back as anyone can remember, there have been stories of many houses in the *Third Ward* being haunted, mostly by peaceful, contented spirits, who seemingly just refuse to leave this world. Others, however, by frantic ghosts trapped somewhere between life and the finality of death. The Wood Mansion is no exception.

"I've been going to the Wood Mansion for years" Francois said, "on a regular basis. I've never seen a ghost or heard anything strange. But that doesn't mean anything. Some people are in tune to those sorts of things, while others aren't."

Local photographer, Greg Geraci, who is well-known in the South Jersey area as the *"Spirit Photographer,"* claims to be very much in tune with the spirit world. Geraci, whose work has been featured in many public displays, has taken dozens of photographs which seemingly depict distinct apparitions. He said he has also captured images of the Virgin Mary and even Jesus through the lens of his camera. Amazingly, one of his photographs shows a very clear image of what can only be described as a UFO. "I couldn't see it when I took the shot, but there it is."

"Things like this happen all the time with me. I feel really blessed to be in touch with the spirit world." Geraci said. He is quite aware of the rumors that the Wood Mansion is haunted, and is not at all surprised. Recently, Geraci walked through the mansion, taking photos and feeling what he called the *"presence of the dead."* as he called it. Upon entering Carrie Wood's old bedroom, he said he immediately felt a warm embrace, as if someone had put their arms around him, a kindred spirit in every way.

"I knew Carrie was there, so I took some pictures," he said. In one of the photos there is a silhouette reflection in her dresser mirror which appears to be eerily shaped like the *"Caroline"* seen in a painting of the lost daughter.

The photographer was asked how many houses he thought were haunted in the Third Ward.

"All of them," Geraci replied,

A Flood of Volunteers

Labor Day, 1930, was supposed to be a day of picnics and family fun in Millville. It was anything but. On Sept. 4, the residents of the city awoke to a blaring, eight-column headline in the Millville Republican: "Flood Danger LESSENS Here: City Divided as Swirling Water Causes Crash of Approaches To Both Bridges Across River." The holiday was spent cleaning up after a very real flood threatened the city.

Recent flooding threatened the structure of the Sharp Street dam that borders the *Third Ward*. And while damage to the dam was considered *very slight* from the flood, it took an *army of volunteers* to ensure there was no real danger. Men and boys from throughout the city worked feverishly to pile sandbags around the channel and sluiceway banks. A portion of the West Side Garage, which was located on the Maurice River, toppled into the water, and many residents were temporarily left without water when a feeder main across from Sharp Street was disabled. The feeder belonged to the Millville Water Company.

"Dawn broke this morning carrying new hope along with a new day for flood-threatened residents of Millville," the paper reported. "City officials and volunteers put through a night of sleepless vigil as six million gallons of turbulent water in Union Lake pounded at the Sharp Street dam, and the churning tide of the Maurice River bit huge chunks out of the shoreline and flooded the meadows. The day marked the crisis of this city's worst flood experience." Some residents had been urged to move to higher ground.

The city was lucky.

According to *The Millville Republican*, "Considering what damage might have been done to Millville by yesterday's serious flood threat, the actual monetary loss was surprisingly small and a casualty list does not exist. This estimate was made by close observers late this morning after it appeared as though the crisis had passed and conditions were returning rapidly to normal.

It continued: "An unofficial estimate of the damage done at the Millville Manufacturing Company sets the figure at less than $10,000." The cost of the damage, however, could rise upon further inspection.

Damage to cottages on Union Lake "is also estimated at a low figure," the paper reported. "Damages to all the cottages are not expected to total more than $3,000."

Some damage was done to stock at the Millville Manufacturing Company, "but the damage is negligible to what it might have been had not the volunteers braced the canal bank and the sluice bank with sand," it was reported. The dam proved to be 'rugged.'

"Millville's dam at Union Lake, built in 1867, held fast all day yesterday even though there was more pressure brought to bear against it than at any time in its long and useful career. The water splashing through its gates at the rate of 50 tons a second shot out 20 feet in the air before it descended."

According to *The Millville Republican*, two U.S. Army Engineers were in Millville later that day. "They merely looked and congratulated officials and volunteers on a job well done."

The flood scare did, however, take a toll on the city. According to the paper, "Approximately 800 employees of the Millville Manufacturing Company will not work today... their inactivity may continue tomorrow but it is hoped and believed that they will be able to return to work by that time."

PART TWO

Optimistic Revival

The Third Ward Today

This brings us up to the present. Just how is the *Third Ward* doing now? Does it deserve the right to keep its nickname *"The Bloody Third?"*

The cotton mill closed in the 1960s leaving many *Third Warders* unemployed. When the glass companies closed in subsequent years, it crippled the employment rate in the *Third Ward*. Some people believe *The Third Ward* – indeed, the city – never recovered. The glass-making glory era in Millville is *all but gone now. At the time of this publication, Millville Chief* Tom Haas had tendered his retirement papers to the city as did Fire Chief Kurt Hess.

Millville Police Chief Jody Farabella, a 17-year member of the force, says he is optimistic about the future of the *Third Ward*. Admittedly, he said, the area is not an ideal place to live right now. "We've had three murders there last year," Farabella said. All three murders were solved. "But honestly, I can't say it's any worse than any other part of the city." The inner parts of Bridgeton-Millville area have seen more than their fair share of shootings in recent years.

"Kidder" Grover Wolverton, Millville Police Department shown here on his motorcycle, early 1930s.

Photo courtesy of Frederick Miller

The city has been plagued with violence, mostly due to the gang activity, Farabella said. A brutal rivalry between The

Bloods and the Gangster Disciples has played a large part in the violence, Farabella said. Arlene Village, which stretched through Archer, Foundry streets and Arnold Drive, was a huge source of the crime problem, he noted. The once-proud apartment complex had deteriorated over the years and morphed into a well-known drug den. The city took steps to demolish the complex and that has eliminated much of the drug   trafficking in that area, Farabella said.

Millville Police Chief Jody Farabella
Photo courtesy Millville Police Department.

them (gangs)," Farabella said. "They don't want to draw attention to themselves. "It (drug trafficking) is a business to them. That area made the community look deplorable."

And while the elimination of Arlene Village has helped tremendously, there still are major problems in *The Third Ward*. Much of the area is considered the *poor* side of town, with more deteriorated houses than well-kept abodes.

The city is constantly cracking down on absentee landlords, said Farabella, himself a landlord who takes his property ownership very seriously. He also noted that in many cases, no matter how well a landlord cares for his property, the renters themselves often neglect the houses and gardens.

The city has become a bit creative in cracking down on neglectful landlords and tenants, using a little-known law called *"excessive use of public services."* That means when police and/or fire personnel are constantly called to the same places time and again, the city can charge them.

Farabella has held several community meetings with *Third Ward* residents. He praised *Third Ward* resident Gladis Mcgraw for rallying the neighbors.

"They are our eyes and ears out there," he said. "They want to fight. They want to stay. Many people have lived there for many years. And they say, 'This is my house. I want to stay.' They say, 'This is my neighborhood, and I'm going to fight for it. And we're going to win this fight.'"

Farabella said that kind of thinking usually happens in pockets of neighborhoods where people have banded together to keep their neighborhoods drug- and crime-free."

He said the city has targeted some drug-ridden hovels for demolition; and that will solve a lot of the problems. A recent ride through *The Third Ward* revealed gap-toothed streets, where problem structures already have been razed.

There is still much to be done, Farabella said. "There are still some *hot spots*, of drugs and violence, but," he said, he is very optimistic about the future not only of *The Third Ward*, but the entire city.

"We have the *Glasstown Arts District* on High Street, which hugs *The Third Ward*. The district is an active hub of painters, writers and a bevy of other vendors, many housed in century-old buildings. What once was a desolate downtown has been transformed into a vibrant area for tourists. The *Third Friday Events* have proved immensely popular.

"I really think things are turning around," Farabella said. "*The Third Ward* has some good roots there. I'd like to see more community policing, but I think things are heading in the right direction. The people there are resilient. They're going to bounce back."

Steve Felice, 47, who served on the MPD from 1990 to 2004, looks back at his time on the Millville streets somewhat differently. He retired from the MPD and is now a detective/sergeant with the Elmer Police Department.

Felice, who has served in numerous positions during his16-year tenure in Millville, has a myriad of awards to his credit. But Felice does have vivid memories of working the *Third Ward* – and he saw the changes first-hand. He served both as a narcotics officer, and in the Major Crimes Unit. Here is his recollection:

"The Third Ward in the early 1990s in my opinion was a mixed bag of everything. What stood out in my mind was a very hard-working, family-oriented neighborhood – a neighborhood where the everyday middle class family would greet you with a hello and a smile. I remember *The Third Ward* as having very narrow streets, with houses very close together and families that were just as close. I remember seeing the kids playing in the (Wood School) school yard and people walking their dogs. I always remember feeling that small-town vibe when I patrolled the streets. I felt like I was home – like this was where I was supposed to be."

But Felice also said he saw a change methodically creep over the *Third Ward* – and not for the better.

Like many other neighborhoods, the *Third Ward* has had its share of crime. "During my 16-years with the Police Department, I have investigated many crimes, ranging from homicides, child abuse, domestic violence, sexual assaults, thefts, burglary and of course the selling of controlled dangerous substance." This was not unique to the *Third Ward*, but the *friendly neighborhoods* of years passed began to morph into something much less friendly.

Felice said: "As the years past, I noticed that the kids weren't playing in the school yard anymore, and the people who once walked their dogs were no longer. This was replaced with drug dealers selling their drugs on the corners and gun shots being fired. This was replaced with mean dogs being trained to fight. The *Third Ward* was no longer the neighborhood I remembered working in."

"A lot of these crimes happened at all times of the day and night," Felice recalled. "I remember working in the Narcotics Unit. " Many of the cases were made from the old Millville Gardens Apartments off Foundry Street. I remember drug deals being made in the Wood School parking lot and thinking to myself : *I can't believe this is happening!* I remember responding to shootings on Archer and Church streets. I remember investigating homicides on Dock and Penn streets. These were just a few that stand out in my mind, when we talk about the *Third Ward*."

And although many Millville residents point to the influx of criminal gangs as the cause of the rise in crime, Detective Felice, someone who has been on the front lines, says that is wrong: "I don't agree. I don't believe that there are any credible organized gangs in the *Third Ward*, or any other part of the city. I believe there are young men and women who have become '*thugs.*' They are misguided people portraying themselves as gang members to feel a sense of belonging. I feel that the number one source of violence is the drug epidemic. I believe that opiates such as heroin and prescription pain killers are contributing to the high crime rate and violence that occurs so frequently throughout the *Third Ward* and surrounding areas."

But Felice, like Farabella, said he sees hope for a good change in the Third Ward. "Being an optimistic person, I believe that the crime rate in the *Third Ward* will only decrease if parents of our younger generation get more involved. Parents need to be held accountable in the teachings of right from wrong. I believe that this new generation of '*police officer*' needs to get out of their patrol cars and walk the streets of the *Third Ward* in order to get a better understanding of the problems. I believe that a community-policing-type program would work well."

In a bit of irony, Felice said: "I believe that if these small changes could be made, then the future for the *Bloody Third Ward* could change to the "*Bloody Third Ward that once was.*"

In 2006, Charles "Bunky" Jones, 43, was shot and killed in his own backyard on Sharp Street in the *Third Ward*. His brother, the Rev. David Ennis, pastor of *In His Presence Worship Center* held rallies to battle violence in the city. Rev. Ennis eventually won a seat on the Millville City Commission, where he continues his mission.

This was once the home of the wildly popular Third Ward Tavern.
Photo by *Charles C. Bennett*

However, no one need look any further than news articles in the local papers and online to conclude that the *Third Ward* is living up to its former nickname, *The Bloody Third*.

Even as this book is being written violent crimes continue. Six men were arrested in connection with the June 2014 shooting of 22-year-old resident James B. Collins of the 10 block of Powell Street early today on the 1000 block of Church Street. It was the second reported incident of gunfire on that block in one week.

The murder was eerily reminiscent of the 1971 Porreco murders in the Third Ward. According to The Press: "Police said that Collins, 22, was fatally shot while running inside a house in the 1000 block of Church Street after gunfire erupted while he was talking to some friends on the front porch around 12:45 a.m."

During the Collins murder, a Church Street resident who declined to be identified, told a South Jersey Times reporter that violence like this has been going on in the *Third Ward* area for some time. "It's turning into worse than *The Bloody Third*," he told the reporter.

The article states that "all six defendants are alleged members or associates of the *Sex, Money, Murder affiliate* of the *Bloods* street gang." The arrests were part of a massive sweep through the city including residents of the *Third Ward* and beyond. The sweep was conducted by local and federal officials, such as the FBI and U.S. Marshalls Fugitive Task Force.

Felice, like Farabella, said he is optimistic when considering the city's popular *Glasstown Arts District*. *The Third Ward* may no longer resemble the friendly neighborhoods of long ago. Subsidized housing is prevalent and many duplexes have been split into apartments. Absentee landlords have added to the downhill spiral of the *Third Ward*. And violence has taken on a new – and much more ubiquitous presence – in the *Third Ward*. Sadly, shootings and other violent acts are not foreign to the *Third Ward* – or the entire city – these days.

Even as this book is being written, there are news reports of a recent shooting in the area of Dock and Foundry streets which left *several* shell casings littering the scene. A report in *The Daily Journal* stated: "Police were dispatched around 8:01 p.m., after multiple 9-1-1 callers reported heavy gunfire in the area. No one was reported injured, and police currently have no suspects."

Speaking with longtime residents of the *Third Ward* today, they all express a common theme: Today the *Third Ward* no longer resembles the friendly neighborhoods of long ago. Subsidized housing is prevalent and many duplexes have been split into apartments. Absentee landlords have added to the downhill spiral of the *Third Ward*. And violence has taken on a new – and much more ubiquitous violence in the *Third Ward* from years past. Many residents in the entire city complain of the escalation of gunfire – whether it is due to gangs or not.

The City's Efforts

Meanwhile, Millville City officials are taking an aggressive approach to cleaning up the *Third Ward*. Efforts to reach Mayor Michael Santiago were not successful. However, City Commissioner Lynne Porreca Compari, director of public affairs explained the city's staunch mission to make the *Third Ward* neighborhood-friendly again.

"We've beefed up code enforcement with a special police officer for the *Third Ward* (and a bit beyond," Compari said. "We've demolished unsafe structures – the ones that are problem areas for police, such as inhabitable homes used as drug dens or squatters. More unsafe structures are scheduled to be razed," she said.

The key to success, Compari said is *follow-up*. Too many landlords – and renters – are ignoring citations by the city to clean up their properties. They're cited, but then there's no follow up. The same thing with the banks. We have a list of banks that have foreclosures. We ask them, 'Ok, you've got X, Y, Z set for foreclosures. What are you going to do about it?' We have to let these people know we're watching. We have to let people know we're following up. People know what they get away with.

"We have wonderful ordinances in place if you just follow them," Compari said.

Working Together

The city is also working with religious and veterans' groups to reclaim the *Third Ward*, Compari said. The two main churches in the *Third Ward* are changing. St. Mary Magdalen Church is now The Parish of All Saints, under the auspices of the Diocese of Camden.

The Second Methodist Church, meanwhile, has been sold to Pastor Ralph Graves and his Cornerstone Church congregation. The former Second Methodist congregation has found another facility. Operating out of the old Blockbuster Video Store on High Street, Compari said Graves's flock bought in the *Third Ward* with the distinct purpose of establishing a presence there. Pastor Graves also bought a half-double on Powell Street – Compari called it '*one of the worst properties*' – and helped renovate it for a single family. Many duplexes had been split into even small apartments, creating a cramped, overcrowded atmosphere. Compari said the city wants to see more single family homes in the *Third Ward*.

Vice Mayor James Quinn agree with Compari. "It's about depopulation," Quinn said of the *Third Ward*. For example, Quinn said, when a quadruple-unit is destroyed by a fire, city commissioners are hoping to replace them with single-family homes. One important step is requiring each housing unit to have a minimum of two on-street parking spaces. Therefore, anyone seeking to rebuild a quadruple complex must have eight on-street parking spaces.

A veterans' group is doing the same thing: Buying a property for a single family – a veteran. The idea is to replace deteriorating duplexes with single family homes, lowering the population in the process.

Another "Bloody Third"

Amazingly, in our travels, we found that Millville wasn't the only city to contain a *"Bloody Third"* ward. According to the website *www.historicthirdward.org*, the town of Milwaukee, Wisconsin, also had a notorious *"Bloody Third Ward,"* although it is now home to an arts and historic district.

The *Third Ward* in Milwaukee is nearly a carbon copy of Millville's. It was a relatively flat, swampy area during its early years. After the land was drained, Irish immigrants settled in the area. Houses covered the east side of the ward, while factories and warehouses were built along the Milwaukee River. The ward developed a reputation for colorful fistfights and soon became known as the *"Bloody Third."*

Wood School Centennial

In 2015, R.D. Wood School began a year-long centennial celebration. Part of the ceremony included *successful Third Warders* who attended the school. They were named to the *Hall of Fame*. On February 15th, students and staffed dressed like it was in 1915. The cornerstone was laid at the school's present location in the *Third Ward* in 1915.

According to a *Bridgeton Evening News* article, the cornerstone was laid on August. 14, 1915. The article reads:

"The laying of the cornerstone of the Richard D. Wood Public School, now in the course of construction on a site bounded by North Powell, Green and Archer streets, in the *Third Ward*, City of Millville, is taking place this afternoon amid elaborate ceremonies conducted by the members of the Junior Order of United American Mechanics."

It is unlikely that Richard Wood envisioned the exceptional alumni that the school which bears his name would have produced. In 2015 alone, five outstanding citizens and former Wood School students were honored for their splendid achievements and contributions to the community. They join dozens of others who have received the *Pride Wall of Fame Award* since 2002, the first year that the honor was given at yearly ceremonies held at RD Wood School.

The 2015 Pride of Fame Recipients at Wood School were honored June 3rd. They are:

Cynthia Lutz Martin, an elementary school teacher in neighboring Haleyville. She is a graduate of Eastern University and Delaware Valley College.

George Kourakin, a popular dentist in Millville, who graduated from the American Academy of Facial Cosmetics.

Matthew Davis who has literally taught school all over the world. He is a graduate of Washington University.

Richard "Dick" Marshall who retired as the Assistant Vice President of Millville National Bank.

Harold Duffield Jr., who went on to excel in law enforcement, working for the Cumberland County Sheriff's Department. He also served as Detective and Sergeant Detective as a member of Community Policing, joining the Millville Police department in 1997.

Other Recipients

2013 – Judy Crowe, Michael Mitchell, Stephanie Perkins, Marquita Evans

2012 – Kenneth Booz, Sr., Matthew Robinson, Katharine Thompson

2011 – James Bacon, Russell Davis, Jr., Bruce Wilson

2008 - John Groth, Paul Roedel, Bonnie Shropshire, Larry Fawcett

2007 – William Fenton, Jr., David Diaz, Christine Ward-Garrison Ph.D, Gregory F. Jacobs, Esq.

2006 – Dr. Richard Beck, Zaklyyah Ennals, Suzanne Merighi, Jeffrey Whiteway

2005 – Anthony Farmer, Jeffrey Joseph, Roger Nathan, Terry Pangburn

2004 – Mathias "Matt" Christy, Walter Clements, Brian Davis, Nicholina Pennington

2003 – Harriet Hogan, Gladis McGraw, Glenn Nickerson, Carrie Parent, Jose Quiles, Meghan Wren

2002 – Brandi Ennals, Leslie Hurley, Rick Morales, Kemble Salvo, Jesse Saterlee

PART THREE

Tidbits

"The Holly City"

In the mid-1900s, the city became known as "The Holly City," because of a businessman's Christmas tradition. Clarence Wolf of New Jersey Silica Sand Company gave Christmas holly boughs from Millville to his delighted patrons. When a spring cold snap threatened the crop, Wolf hired horticulturist Daniel Fenton to oversee the holly population. It was a huge success, with holly bushes adorning nearly every area of the city. In 1951, Millville officially became known as "The Holly City."

Abbott's Bakery

Brothers Robert and Richard Abbott lived on W. Green Street from 1924-1928. They attended Wood School, like all the other Third Warders. The brothers were bakers in the service during WWII. After the war, they returned to Millville and started Abbott's Bakery. People flocked to High Street for what were arguably the best pies, cakes and cookies ever baked in the region.

"We had a lot of customers from the *Third Ward*. Could have been maybe most of our customers came from there, early on. Good people, tough and honest. Most everybody walked to the bakery back then, up until about the sixties," said Robert Abbott's son, also named Robert. The day the bakery closed in 1994 was a day of near-mourning in the city.

Miss Millville

Mary Marie Stites, 96, of Bridgeton, was a young lady by the last name of *Terzes* when she captured the *Miss Millville* crown decades ago.

Mary Marie Terzes was a proud resident of the *Third Ward*, and she had snagged several other beauty contest crowns. "She was quite pretty," said her daughter, Mary Jane Moats, who lived on Green Street, then Church Street, until she left in 1964.

Moats said she has researched long and hard trying to find photos of her mother as Miss Millville, but hasn't had any luck yet. At a spritely 96, she still talks about having won the coveted contest, today.

"She won a refrigerator," her daughter said. "That was a big deal back then – she was so happy! The *new-fangled* food cooler meant no more 'ice deliveries' for her family."

Moats recalled that her mother was not very healthy as a child, and her parents tried to keep her indoors and calm. But Mary Marie would have none of that. She became an active participant in shows at the Levoy Theater, and entered several beauty pageants, always winning one prize or another, according to her daughter.

The Shy Artist

The art of mold-making at the Millville glass industry proved to be a source of inspiration for one local artist. Donald Harris Breeden, a man of many talents, painted a magnificent portrait of a mold maker's hands at work. It was painted in the 1960s. His daughter, Judith Breeden McFarland, said that her father – who died eight years ago at the age of 94 – "was a great artist, although he only did it as a hobby."

"He lived at 317 Sassafras St. He worked for Whitall Tatum, Armstrong Cork and Maul Brothers, where he became an industrial engineer, designing the machines that made the glass bottle," Judith said. He was quite the character. "He also was an early aviator. He and his brother and a cousin built a glider from a kit," she said. "They had someone tow them down Rieck Avenue by car and then when it became airborne, the rope was dropped."

Out the Window!

Gloria Treen McKenzie said: "My parents owned the house next to the (Wood) school playground. They used to call it the *'Bloody Third.'* I know it wasn't the best place. I even remember one night a man climbed through a window as my mom slept on the sofa. She screamed and scared him so bad that he fell out of the window! We still laugh about it. That was about 1970 at 620 Dock Street."

Arlene Village, Then and Now

JoAnn Wyjadka Candy said: "I lived in Arlene Village in the 1960s. I have fond memories of the neighbors and the little play area outside my front door. It was in the late 1990s or early 2000s. I took my sons back to my hometown to show them around. I remember rolling up to 13A Arnold Drive, getting out of the car and looking around, pointing out where the slide was and looking for a holly bush.

"Going back to the car, I noticed a small group in front of the Laundromat. I introduced myself and explained that I was just looking around at the home I grew up in. Only one person even *looked* at me, and she said something about how '*things get out of hand.*'

"After we got back in the car, I noticed that most of the neighbors had baseball bats and I had unwittingly walked into a neighborhood dispute. As I drove out I could hear police sirens coming. I have since learned that Arlene Village has been bulldozed."

Seasonal Fun

Carol Uminski Rose: "Probably my three most favorite memories of growing up in Millville is: On snowy days, when school was called off, we would walk along the high snow banks along Main Street with our tied-together ice skates slung over our shoulders and head down to Hankins Pond. We sometimes would have a bonfire there to warm up, in between skating.

The boat houses at Union Lake Park were a summer play refuge for children throughout the city, especially ones from the Third Ward.
Photo Courtesy of Dale Weinstein.

"Also I remember my two best friends and me on a banana seat Stingray bike heading to Franks or McCloskey's store for popsicles on a hot summer day – summer days at Union Lake where we had a cottage. We would run around the woods, swim whenever and wherever we wanted! We practically lived in our 'bathing' suits, pick wild blueberries (huckleberries? for our big sister to bake something for us.

"We'd be eating watermelons outside on a stool and spitting the seeds in a small shrub bed outside the back door; shelling Lima beans there too. Dad would be cooking out on our stone grill out back, sneaking into the 'Canoe Club,' later called the 'Sailing Club' for sodas and to watch the older girls taking baton twirling lessons (what I aspired to do when I grew up); yelling 'Geronimo!' as we ran, with our dog, and charged into the lake; walking down to Dix's (Aunt Becky's) for ice cream after dinner. Mom and Dad would send us to get the house to themselves for a while. They always told us to stop and see Linda and Bloomie (Phrampus).

"I remember taking swimming lessons from Axel Johnson. It was a great place, and time, to grow up!" Rose said.

Swinging the night away at a YMCA dance in 1960.

Photo Courtesy of Dale Weinstein.

Snow Days

Cheryl Justice of California said, "I lived on Powell Street when I was a kid in the early 70s. The snow plows would push the snow against the fence at Wood School. We kids would play for hours pretending the heaps of snow were mountains. We would build forts and have snowball fights. I moved to California 35 years ago but will always remember those carefree days of my childhood."

Third Ward Roots

Paula Simpkins Maitre said, "My great grandparents (Aaron and Elizabeth Simpkins) and my Grandfather Fred lived on McNeal Street in the late 1800s. Elizabeth worked in the cotton mill, and Aaron in the glass house on S. Second Street. Later they moved to the west side.

Rebels

Chrissy Jeffery said,
"I remember riding my bike through the trail to sneak into Wheaton Village by the playground. It made Jamie Jones (now Jamie Slimmer) and I feel like rebels to do that!" They lived around the corner from Wheaton Village.

'Mother, May I?'

Carole Barber said she lived at High and Green Streets.

"I had the happiest childhood ever! Roller skating, playing with all the neighborhood kids until the street lights came on. Games were "Mother May I?"; "Hide and Seek," "Jacks;" etc. There was nothing ever to fear. Everyone looked out for all the kids.

I could go on and on but will just say I wish my grandkids could have had such great morning play-times as we did growing up in the *Third Ward.*"

A Mini-Paradise

Adrienne Treadway Shorter recalls the *Third Ward* as a kind of mini-paradise growing up. I remember a small park on North Street, near Foundry. I used to play there in the early 60's, between the Lacivita's and Goldies' stores. Those were the good ol' days when we could walk to those parks and our parents not worry. My parents and grandparents lived on Church Street. Joan Lacivita is my aunt, so I was all over that neighborhood.

I wouldn't let my children or grandchildren out of my sight nowadays!"

The Stuffed Bobcat

Harry Fisher asked:

"Anyone remember the bobcat that was killed at Union Lake back in the '60s? My mom does. She saw it in front of our house at 196 Sharp St. a week before they shot it.

Terry Pangburn remembers it well:

"Franklin Menz bought that bobcat and had it stuffed. It was in his restaurant when it was on Delsea Drive. I remember it well, but I thought that it was killed in the Cumberland area."

Enduring Friendships

(At Right) Third Ward pals, Carl "Buddy" Abdel, Chick Bennett and Sam Bennett reunite for old times in the 1990s.

Third Ward buddies, Carl "Buddy" Abdel, Chick Bennett and Sam Bennett in June 1948.

The Archer Street Tree

Kathy Powell Horner has an unusual memory about her childhood in the *Third Ward*.

"When I was in Wood School, if I got a 'D' or an 'F' grade on a paper, there used to be a tree that had a big hole in it that all the kids would throw their bad papers in. The tree was on Archer Street."

One Tough Cookie

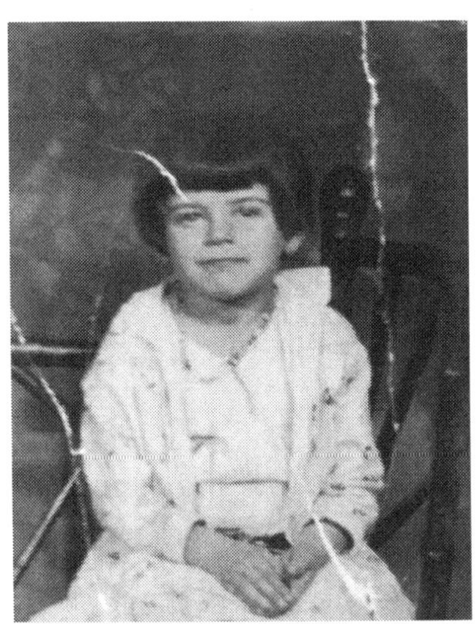

Andrea Scott said her mother, Blanche Herman, grew up in the *Bloody Third.* *Blanch* claimed she could beat up any boy. "She was a real spicy gal!" Scott said. She often had the battle scars to prove it, around 1932 when both of her knees frequently sported scabs.

Blanche Herman, who grew up in the "Bloody Third,"
claimed she could beat up any boy.

Photo courtesy of Andrea Scott

Epilogue

The Third Ward, sadly, has seen a steady decline over the years. It no longer resembles the homes of hard-working shift glassmakers or cotton mill workers. Many of the homes have been divided into apartments.

But Millville city officials optimistically feel they have finally laid out a realistic plan to return the neighborhood to a semblance of its former glory. By actively attacking problem houses, and working to keep the population down, city officials feel they finally will be able to make some concrete changes.

The Third Ward may never return to the *glory days* of the glass factories or cotton mills, but there seems to be a good chance it will once again be a neighborhood residents will be proud to call *home* again.

Other Select Books Published by Fireside Publications

Available at: www.firesidepubs.com or
Amazon.com; Kindle; Nook

The Crystal Angel	Olivia Claire High
The Rose Cottage	Olivia Claire High
Dreams: Shadows of the Night	Olivia Claire High
A Stranger's Eyes	Olivia Claire High
The Wolf Deception	Olivia Claire High
Kari's Destiny: No More Tomorrows	Olivia Claire High
Essays: On Living with Alzheimer's Disease:	
The First Twelve Months	Lois Wilmoth-Bennett
The Furax Connection	Stephen L. Kanne
The Find	James J. Valko
Above Honor: Rachel's Story	Donald Himelstein
Beyond Forever	Taylor Shaye
The Cleansing	Dr. Ben F. Eller
The Death of Learning	Dr. Ben F. Eller
18 Days in September	Allen N. Hunt, Ph.D
Independence Day Plague	Carla Lee Suson
Odds & Ends ~Bits & Pieces	Joye O'Keefe
The Serpent Sea	Linda Lehmann Masek
Where Danger Lurks	Judith Groudine Finkel
Texas Justice	Judith Groudine Finkel
Ice Rose	Alison Neuman
Searching for Normal: A Memoir	Alison Neuman
Raven April	Nelson Trout
Amanda's Voice	Eileen Bennett
Silver Strands	Eileen Bennett

Made in the USA
Lexington, KY
10 January 2016